Do-able Differentiation

*Varying Groups, Texts,
and Supports to Reach Readers*

Michael F. Opitz and Michael P. Ford

HEINEMANN
Portsmouth, NH

Heinemann
361 Hanover Street
Portsmouth, NH 03801–3912
www.heinemann.com

Offices and agents throughout the world

The general teaching suggestions, key elements, and intermediate grade lessons shown in Chapters 3 through 6 are adaptations of material found in Michael P. Ford's *Differentiation Through Flexible Grouping: Successfully Reaching All Readers*, © 2005. Naperville, IL: Learning Point Associates.

Library of Congress Cataloging-in-Publication Data
Opitz, Michael F.
   Do-able differentiation : varying groups, texts, and supports to reach readers / Michael F. Opitz, Michael P. Ford.
       p.   cm.
   Includes bibliographical references and index.
   ISBN-13: 978-0-325-01283-4
   ISBN-10: 0-325-01283-0
   1. Individualized reading instruction.   I. Ford, Michael P.   II. Title.   III. Title: Doable differentiation.
LB1573.45.O65 2008
372.41'7—dc22   2008004609

Editor: Kate Montgomery
Production: Vicki Kasabian
Cover design: Jenny Jensen Greenleaf
Typesetter: Kim Arney
Manufacturing: Louise Richardson

Printed in the United States of America on acid-free paper
12 11 10 09 08 ML 1 2 3 4 5

CONTENTS

Acknowledgments vii
Introduction ix

1 Understanding How Readers Differ and Teachers Matter 1

2 Grouping Structures Overview 23

3 Model 1: Grouping Without Tracking 31

4 Model 2: Jigsawing 51

5 Model 3: Connected Literature Circles 69

6 Model 4: Focused Readers' Workshop 93

7 Yeah . . . But . . . What About These Questions? 112

Appendix A: Bibliography of Professional Resources 129
Appendix B: Blank Lesson Plan Forms 135
Children's Literature Cited 140
References 141
Index 144

We would like to acknowledge the inspirational words of Dick Allington who we first heard say: "Kids differ. Teachers matter," which we have liberally borrowed for the theme of this book. We would also like to acknowledge the role of the many individuals at Heinemann: editors Tina Miller and Kate Montgomery who were willing to travel far and wide leading us to this project instead of the project they were originally hoping for; Jillan Scahill for tidying up some loose ends; Vicki Kasabian for turning the manuscript into the book you see here; Eric Chalek for his writing what appears on the back cover; Jenny Jensen Greenleaf for the cover design; Denise Botelho, whose copyediting insights brought greater clarity; Cindy Black for her proofreading talent; Kim Arney, who typeset this book with great care and a superb design sense; Alex Murray for his index; and Louise Richardson, who handled the manufacture of this book. Our thanks to Charlene Cobb and Danielle Carnahan of Learning Point Associates who provided a forum for first organizing these thoughts and ideas; Melanie Sickinger and the Wrightstown (WI) School District for allowing use of their Response to Intervention plan; Maria Graf and the Clintonville (WI) School District for insights and ideas for working with ELLs; Jennifer A. Davis, doctoral candidate at the University of Northern Colorado who crafted the lesson annotations; our colleagues at the University of Northern Colorado and the University of Wisconsin–Oshkosh for their ongoing support of our professional endeavors; and to our families for sacrifices they made as we completed this work.

You can boil the last fifty years of educational research down to four words—
Kids differ, teachers matter.

—Richard Allington, *What Really Matters for Struggling Readers*

We all want children to be the best readers possible, don't we? It is this desire that keeps us searching for ways to reach them, *all* of them, isn't it? And it is this search that takes us to professional conferences and to professional texts (both print and electronic), right? Invariably, though, our searching leads us to more than one answer and we are left on our own to synthesize and internalize them so that we can apply what we know for the sake of our students. Take differentiated reading instruction, the topic of this book, for example. It seems as though nearly every educational publisher of professional books has at least one text related to differentiated instruction. Taken together, these publications offer an array of ideas about what differentiated instruction should entail, from addressing gender to multiple intelligences, not to mention learning styles and personality types. While the authors of these texts approach differentiation from a different vantage point, as a group they underscore a major point we make in this text and a point that teachers focused on children's learning rather than a prescribed curriculum have long known: *readers differ.*

And, thanks to the work of researchers such as Wharton-McDonald, Pressley, and Hampston (1998), we now have even more evidence to support a second point we make in this book and one that practicing teachers know firsthand: *teachers matter.* Indeed, we have much to celebrate in light of these findings. And now more than ever before, many different kinds of activities should show themselves in classrooms as a way of honoring readers' differences while at the same time providing anecdotal evidence that knowledgeable teachers are crafting their lessons with reader differences in mind.

What should exist, however, and what actually exists is quite different. Even though there is much talk given to differences, for example, teachers more often than not are expected to follow lockstep curricula and are often monitored to make sure that they are being true to the program (i.e., high fidelity). Another reason for the difference between espoused and applied ideas stems from the writing about differentiation itself. Because there are so many perspectives on differentiation, teachers can become confused and overwhelmed and then are inclined to shut down rather than open up to manageable ways to address readers' differences. Frustration can triumph over action for busy, caring teachers who are trying to survive the many mandates imposed on them. So while differentiation is at the heart of helping all children become the best possible readers, there seems to be little or no time to sort out all of the information about differentiation. Yet, given all we know about reader differences and how paying attention to them will better ensure that children advance as readers, we have little choice. We are called on to eke out some time to attend to it. Clearly, understanding and applying differentiated instruction is simply too important to leave unattended.

That's where this book comes into play. In writing it, we reviewed a tremendous amount of information about differentiation. We also thought about and discussed our own teaching experiences, regardless of grade level. Finally, we consulted newer legislation aimed at helping to ward off reading problems as early as possible (e.g., Response to Intervention). All of this knowledge led us to include the information that now forms the content of this book. Our aim is to show and tell you ways to take much of what is known about differentiation and use it in practical and manageable ways. In fact, as you'll see in the sample lessons we provide and their accompanying explanations, differentiation fits easily into an already existing classroom routine. You are probably doing more differentiating than you realize and these lessons will help you to become more aware of how you might be differentiating and ways that you can enhance those practices.

In Chapter 1, we provide some background about differing differentiation perspectives. We discuss what the different perspectives have in common as well as how they differ. We then share our beliefs about differentiation. We continue by offering some suggestions about how to use much of the information garnered from these different perspectives in practical ways. For instance, rather than encouraging you to administer, score, and analyze the many different kinds of learning styles inventories, as suggested by some proponents of that perspective, we instead suggest that you use your time more wisely by assuming that there are many reader differences and use what you know about these possible differences when designing instruction. Your lesson then reflects different modalities, learner preferences, and intelligences so that by the end of the lesson, you will have addressed most if not all learner differences somewhere in the lesson. We conclude this chapter by making the case for using four specific grouping structures as a practical way to hone in on reader differences when engaging children with texts for in so doing, we are convinced that you will better succeed in reaching all readers.

In Chapters 2 through 6, we provide information about the different grouping models. We provide an overview of the models in Chapter 2. In Chapter 3, we explain a grouping without tracking model whereas in Chapter 4 we discuss a jigsawing model. In Chapter 5, we elaborate on a connected literature circles model and, in Chapter 6, we zoom in on a focused readers' workshop model. Each chapter follows the same format:

- Diagram of the model

- Scenario

- Explanation

- Key Elements

- General Teaching Suggestions for . . .

  • preparing the lesson

  • frontloading

  • reading and responding

  • extending

- A Sample Lesson for Primary Grades

- A Sample Lesson for Intermediate Grades

- Additional Resources

Many times, the differentiated instruction we suggest in this book calls for some children to work independently. As we have discussed in other publications, when children are working away from the teacher, they need to be engaged with meaningful literacy activities that will enhance their understanding of how language works. They also need to be taught how to work independently. In Chapter 7, we offer some suggestions to help you know just what to do with the rest of the students when you are working with a small group.

We close the book with appendices that you can use to extend your understanding of this book in one way or another. Appendix A lists additional professional references and Appendix B provides blank lesson planning forms that can be reproduced for your own use.

Not sure where to begin? As a way of showing you as much as telling you about differentiated instruction, here's what we propose. First, start with Chapter 1 so that you can gain an understanding of differentiation as we see it. This understanding will serve as a foundation as you read the remaining chapters. Second, take a look at Chapter 2 as it will provide you with an overview of the grouping structures, how they are alike and different. Third, preview the remaining chapters. Beyond this preview, though, differentiation kicks into high gear. If you are new to using different grouping structures in your classrooms, especially as a way to emphasize reader differences, we suggest that you begin with Chapter 3, "Grouping Without Tracking," and once you feel you have a good handle on it, move to the next chapter. Continue in this sequential manner because each model becomes increasingly more complex and each of the previous models serves as a scaffold for the models that follow it. Following this sequence and moving along when you feel you and your students are ready, you move at your own pace, one that ensures success for both you and your students.

Others of you might already be somewhat familiar and comfortable with the models we present. However, you may be looking to refine one or more of the models so that you can better emphasize differentiation. You might also be looking for ways to improve your use of the grouping structures. In this case, we suggest that you begin with the model you most want to refine and move to the others as you see fit. Keep in mind that we wrote Chapters 3 through 6 as stand-alone chapters so that we could better help you read the chapters in the manner that best fits your needs. You might not need the same level of support as other readers and therefore need not follow any specific chapter sequence.

Still others of you might be comfortable with most of the models to the point where you would like to challenge yourself to try another way of reaching readers. We suggest that you try out one that is new to you. Many teachers, for example, like the idea of a readers' workshop yet shy away from it because they are unsure how they can manage it. The focused readers' workshop model we explain in Chapter 6 might be just the way to embrace the challenge and to forge ahead.

Regardless of the order you choose to read the chapters, reading and digesting them all will better enable you to understand and to provide differentiated instruction as we define it in this text. As a result of reading this text and reflecting on your own teaching experiences, we are confident that you will agree with the major point we make in this text which is this: *readers differ and teachers matter!*

Understanding How Readers Differ and Teachers Matter

We agree with Allington. Our own teaching experiences, past and present, across a variety of grade levels kindergarten to college, give us firsthand evidence that readers differ, regardless of age. And, once again, we can draw on our own experiences as ample evidence that teachers matter. All children need a teacher who knows how to target instruction effectively and how to accommodate learners' differences in that classroom. Every child needs a teacher who knows how to differentiate reading instruction.

What Is Differentiated Instruction?

Ask different teachers and researchers this question, and you are sure to receive different answers. Tomlinson (1999) defines it as a teacher's response guided by general principles such as respectful tasks, flexible grouping, and ongoing assessment and adjustment through which teachers vary content, process, and products according to students' readiness, interest, and learning profiles through a range of instructional management strategies. Others suggest that it is instruction geared toward helping all children, regardless of perceived reading level, advance as readers. The instruction provided them is steered and monitored by assessment (Walpole and McKenna 2007). Still others see it as a means of recognizing that all brains are unique and, therefore, require a variety of learning options including varying the amount of time to complete a task, learning modalities, social conditions, complexity of the content, and available resources (Jensen 2007). Yet another definition encompasses the affective need of students that "inspires feelings of safety, comfort, excitement, motivation, and satisfaction" (Schwartz and Kluth 2007, vi). Regardless of definition, a common thread that ties them together is the underlying belief that differentiated instruction is both a philosophy of and technique for instruction that defies a one-size-fits-all approach to teaching and learning. Differentiation champions an atmosphere in which teachers "strive to do whatever it takes to ensure that [all students] grow as much as they possibly can each day, each week, and throughout the year" (Tomlinson 1999, 2). We subscribe to this belief while at the same time recognize that there is more than one way for this differentiation to play out.

But we caution that just because there are many paths to differentiated instruction, that doesn't mean every path leads to differentiated instruction. This may be especially true when we apply these many different differentiation insights specifically to elementary reading programs. We simply cannot, for example, purchase a differentiation reading kit that contains a prescribed sequence of lessons to be completed with all learners, regardless of context, if we want to reach all readers. Instead, we need to develop, in Tomlinson's words, "a consistent, robust plan in anticipation of and in response to students' learning differences" (9). This is akin to the kind of instruction set forth in the recent Response to Intervention (RTI) initiative. In essence, the most recent reauthorization of the Individuals with Disabilities Education Improvement Act (IDEA) calls on all educators to devise a consistent plan (e.g., standard protocol or problem-solving protocol) to respond to each child's unique needs as early as possible in an effort to ward off potential reading problems from the start.

We also want to caution about a vision of differentiation in its purest form that suggests a degree of complexity that would be impossible to achieve. Paying attention to multiple intelligences alone in every decision about content, process, or products would keep any teacher busy enough, let alone incorporating additional ways to differentiate instruction. (See Figure 1–1.) Think of pure differentiation as a multiplication problem in which you factor in two genders, four learning styles, and eight ways of thinking. The answer leaves you with the potential of identifying sixty-four different learning profiles especially when you consider different content and contexts. Now imagine being ready and able to address all of these profiles throughout the day. You get the idea. Doing so would be very unlikely. We agree with Tomlinson when she states, "the teacher does not try to differentiate everything for everyone every day. That's impossible" (14).

That being said, a close examination of different differentiation models displayed in Figure 1–1 shows the many potential ways that they can be combined to create a differentiated classroom. And even though our interaction with children helps us to see that they are differentiation blends rather than differentiation singles, just how to remember and apply this understanding in

Figure 1–1 *Ways to Think About Differentiation*

Differentiation Orientation	Brief Explanation	Citations
Learning Styles	Learners learn through different modalities: auditory, visual, tactile, kinesthetic.	Dunn and Dunn (1987)
	Learners can be "categorized" according to experiential learning: • Accommodators • Convergers • Assimilators • Divergers	Kolb (1984)
	Learners are grouped in the 4MAT model: • Innovative learner • Analytical learner • Commonsense learner • Dynamic learner	McCarthy (2006)
	Learners are divided by their type of thought processes: • Mastery (recall) • Interpersonal (relate personally) • Self-expressive (reorganize) • Understanding (reason)	Silver, Strong, and Perini (2000)
Thinking Styles	Learners have different ways of thinking: • Concrete Random • Concrete Sequential • Abstract Sequential • Abstract Random	Gregoric (1982)
	Learners use information in practical, analytical, and creative ways, which is a hallmark of successful people.	Sternberg (1996)
	Learners possess multiple intelligences: • Verbal/Linguistic • Intrapersonal • Logical/Mathematical • Visual/Spatial • Interpersonal • Bodily/Kinesthetic • Musical/Rhythmic • Naturalist	Gardner (1983)
Affective Styles	Learners' emotional intelligences include the ability to self-motivate, be persistent, control impulses, regulate mood, and have empathy and hope.	Goleman (1995)
	Habits of Mind describe a character-centered view of intelligence including sixteen habits ranging from listening empathetically to responsible risk taking; from managing impulsively to responding with wonderment and awe.	Costa and Kallick (2000)
Developmental Levels	Children are in a constant state of learning to be literate. This development includes an increasing understanding of linguistic, cognitive, and sociocultural literacy processes and strategies. Development continues throughout one's life as literacy is used in new and different ways (e.g., new literacies).	Kucer (2005)

a manageable way is the challenge. We propose the four grouping models that form the larger part of this book as a convenient and practical way to apply this understanding because they fit into the already existing classroom reading instruction routines. We also propose these grouping models in this way because they enable us to apply our differentiated instruction beliefs in a sensible, doable manner.

What Are Our Beliefs About Differentiated Instruction?

Like others who write about differentiation (e.g., Wormeli 2007), we base our view on a set of beliefs. They stem from our combined sixty-year teaching experiences that span teaching grade levels from kindergarten through college, with novice and practicing teachers alike. They also come from extensive professional reading and writing and from examining our own learning preferences. But as important to our understanding of differentiation comes from our being fathers, two sons apiece. We live differentiation at home as well as at school.

Belief #1: Differentiation During Reading Instruction Needs to Address the Complex Relationship Among Four Critical Elements: Reader, Text, Activity, and Context

Years ago, Clay (1991) noted that to help readers advance, teachers needed to pay attention to the interaction among the text, reader, and context for it is only then that they can better understand what a child knows and needs to know. This knowing then enables teachers to design appropriate instruction. We could not agree more. Taking a look at each of these elements is critical to better understand this complex relationship.

Every time reading instruction takes place, four critical elements are interacting and variation in any one of those element changes the potential impact of the instruction. First is the *reader*. As we have shown in the previous explanation, readers differ in one of several ways. Each brings a different set of characteristics (e.g., level of motivation, vocabulary, general knowledge, purpose for reading, views of reading) to the reading table and the text that awaits reading instruction. When we consider the potential variation in these readers' characteristics and also think about differences due to gender, age, languages, and learning abilities, we begin to see just how much variation can exist among readers themselves.

Second is the *text*. Each text—or even part of a text—carries with it its own set of demands for readers. Authors use different content, concepts, formats, organization, and purposes when they construct the text and even without authorial intention, the texts themselves hold meaning for readers. Variation in any text factor can make a text more difficult or easier to read.

Third is the instructional reading *activity(ies)* used during reading instruction. When selecting activities with student success in mind, several questions surface: What is the task? What is the outcome? How should students be grouped? How much teacher support will be needed?

Fourth is the *context*. All reading instruction takes place in a context. There is a physical setting for the reading instruction, which includes environmental factors that contribute to or impede successful reading instruction. There is also a metaphysical setting for the reading instruction in which a variety of psychological, sociological, cultural, and political factors interact with the other elements.

Acknowledging the complex interaction of these four elements during reading instruction underscores the importance of teachers who understand the complexity and can use their understanding to help maximize students' reading potential. In other words, while teachers may not be able to control the individual differences students bring to the instructional setting, they often do have some control over which texts to use with given students, the activities used with those students, and how to establish a nurturing instructional environment. The teacher who acts on what he or she knows about

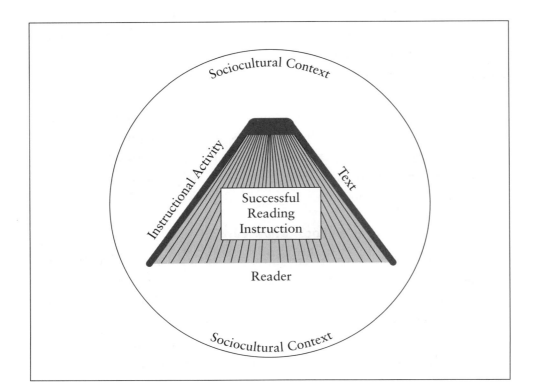

these elements is what enables differentiated reading instruction. So not only do readers differ; teachers matter.

Belief #2: Differentiation Should Target Key Outcomes of a Balanced Literacy Program That Includes Local, Global, and Affective Knowledge of Reading

Considering all the ways that readers can and do differ can lead teachers to feel overwhelmed and frustrated rather than in control and at ease. The constraints of the classroom preclude addressing every possible difference. So what are teachers to do? First and foremost, remember that we, like our students, need to feel successful. Said another way, no one likes to go home at the end of the day feeling like a total failure. Start by thinking of a few specific, realistic target outcomes, goals you can get your hands and mind around. And thanks to the help of Fitzgerald (1999), teachers can set realistic goals. In her article, "What Is This Thing Called 'Balance'?" Fitzgerald identifies three critical reader outcomes of a balanced literacy program: local, global, and affective knowledge of reading. *Local knowledge* of the print is the reader's knowledge of letters and sounds, word parts, words, sentence structures, and literal comprehension. The learner must be able to handle the print at this micro level. *Global knowledge* of print describes the strategies readers use to address larger chunks of texts and the ability to understand and respond to the texts. So not only do learners need to be able to handle print at the micro level, they also need to handle it at the macro level. *Affective knowledge* of reading is also important. Learners need to be able to handle not only the cognitive demands of the reading process but also the affective demands of being a reader. Fitzgerald emphasizes that these three key outcomes are not discrete, but instead overlap and often impact one another. At a minimum, then, teachers need to recognize the potential differences in learners in three knowledge areas: local, global, and affective. Taking a closer look at each area promises to help teachers better understand how to apply them to the program and differentiate along the way.

How Do Students Differ on Local Knowledge?

It may be obvious that learners can differ in their local knowledge. We know students may know different letters, sounds, words, and strategies to handle print at a local level. Often these differences are ignored when instruction is provided in groups. Needs are collapsed and generalized across the groups. While some students sit and receive instruction about things they need, others may sit and listen to things they already know while their needs go unattended. Students are grouped by arbitrary levels during guided reading even though their word strategy needs might be quite different. Students who are at different stages of spelling development are all placed in the same spelling program, with whole classes engaged in making words, building word families by analogy, or working through letter-of-the-week activities. What's going on here? The better question may be: What isn't?

In situations like these, little is being done to address learner differences. Yet so much more could happen with some differentiation. When a child reads aloud, one of five typical patterns happens. (See Figure 1–2.) First, the reading is read correctly. Second, the reading is not initially read correctly, but almost all miscues are self-corrected. Third, the reading is comprehended even though some miscues are not self-corrected. Fourth, the reading is attempted but it is clear that meaning making has not taken place.

Figure 1–2 *Five Typical Reading Performance Patterns*

Reader Performance	What pattern would teachers observe?	What is working?	What needs to be worked on?	What else should be considered?
Correct	Accurate	The reader is reading with confidence, comfort, and competence.	Consider adjusting the expectations for the reader.	Is the material being read an appropriate match? What are the instructional goals for the reader?
Corrected	Accurate but with self-corrections.	The reader is monitoring meaning and adjusting when errors are made.	Look closely at self-corrections to see what cueing strategies might need to be strengthened.	What does the reader need to be more accurate as he or she makes meaning?
Comprehended	Meaning-based miscues.	The reader is making sense as he or she reads.	The reader may need to focus more closely on using graphophonemic and visual cues.	Does the reader need to slow down, be more accurate with decoding, and/or more balanced in his or her strategy use?
Attempted	Nonmeaning-based miscues.	The reader is taking risks with reading.	The reader may need to focus closely on using semantic and syntactic cues.	Is the reader relying too much on decoding to the detriment of comprehension and fluency? Does the reader need to be more accurate as he or she makes meaning?

Finally, the reading might break down or stall. The teacher's response needs to depend on the pattern that the teacher observes.

Consider the following scenario, which illustrates why differentiation is so important. Imagine two students reading the predictable story *The Merry-Go-Round* by Jillian Cutting (Wright Group, 1998). Both students have been placed in the same reading group because they are at the same level according to their accuracy scores taken from a running record.

The first child reads the story and makes seven miscues substituting *chimp* for *monkey* (twice), *hippo* for *hippopotamus* (twice), and *alligator* for *crocodile* (three times). The second child reads the same story and also makes seven miscues. The child omits *hippopotamus* (twice), substitutes *money* for *monkey* (twice), and mispronounces *crocodile* (three times). Now let's look closely at these two readers who are in the same leveled guided reading group. If you look at their accuracy level with this text, the two readers are exactly the same. Each has seven miscues for an accuracy level of about 89 percent. Likewise, if we look just at the words they missed, these two readers look exactly the same. They each missed *monkey, hippopotamus,* and *crocodile* the same number of times. But the assumption that the same instruction is needed to help them handle text at the local level falls apart when one looks at the actual miscues each child made. The child who substituted *chimp* for *monkey, hippo* for *hippopotamus,* and *alligator* for *crocodile* was clearly making meaning as the reading took place. The child who substituted *money* for *monkey,* skipped *hippopotamus,* and mispronounced *crocodile* was struggling to make meaning as the reading took place. So depending on the purpose for grouping these two readers together, they may be in the wrong group. For example, the first child comprehended the story but did not read with complete accuracy. The second child attempted the story but did not comprehend. In targeting instruction, each child would need to be reached with a different response.

Knowing something about readers' *local knowledge* and using it when looking at readers' performances will more likely lead you to target the needed instruction for all learners. Indeed, exemplary teachers who have the greatest impact on performance and achievement appear to be able to do this kind of analysis (Pressley 2005).

How Do Students Differ on Global Knowledge?

High-stakes tests are alive and well in the new millennium, and students are often labeled "struggling readers" when they fail to pass them. Debates about the types and purposes of assessments aside, an enormous problem with emphasizing students' overall scores from any single test is that students are often lumped into one of two groups: those who can meet the standards and those who can't. As if this isn't problematic enough, what then often occurs is that once sorted, students in the latter group are often given the same kind of instruction, when in reality there is much variation among them. When this instruction fails some children, well-meaning educators are often surprised and express wonderment about why all children are not succeeding. Enter researchers such as Valencia and Buly (2004) to shed some light on what might be happening. As a result of giving each failing student three additional reading assessments, they discovered that students who fall below the high-stakes testing standard had different reasons for doing so. Equipped with their findings, Valencia and Buly identified six different reader profiles. They also provide some concrete suggestions to assist teachers in teaching readers similar to each profile, putting differentiated reading instruction within reach. These are shown as reader strategy profiles in Figure 1–3.

Valencia's and Buly's research reminds teachers that even with a minimal amount of analysis, readers differ. Instead of looking for one right way to help all students meet the standard (if that needs to be our goal), we need to look for as many different ways as possible to help those students. Teachers need to focus their time and energy on targeting the right intervention to the right student. This kind of differentiation in the reading program will pay off and students will benefit.

How Do Students Differ on Affective Knowledge?

In *Books and Beyond* (Opitz and Ford 2006), we discuss at length the importance of using a variety of texts to capitalize on researchers' findings about the affective side of reading. That discussion still holds and so we summarize it here.

In 1997, Guthrie and Wigfield reported on their study that was designed to look at readers' motivation. They concluded that motivation is multifaceted and complex; it can be described as affect, involvement, and/or interest, and varies across different classroom contexts. Two years later, Baker and Wigfield (1999) reported the findings on their study, which they designed to look closely at this issue. Acknowledging that motivation is multidimensional, they assessed readers using a scale with multiple motivation variables. They looked at eleven variables (self-efficacy, grades, curiosity, recognition, compliance, involvement, challenge, importance, competition, social, and work avoidance). Baker and Wigfield discovered that a combination of factors influenced the affective dimensions of a reader. They also identified seven motivational profiles of readers (see Figure 1–4). Examining these profiles can help teachers target efforts better as they try to motivate students.

Figure 1-3 *Reader Strategy Profiles*

Reader Profile	Accuracy	Rate	Comprehension	Reader Challenges	Intervention Ideas
1. Slow Steady Comprehenders	OK	Slow	Weren't able to answer all questions but all answered were answered correctly	Given that these students are able to say the words accurately and show that they understand what they have read, they may need to learn how to adjust reading rate to purpose.	• Provide students with help in understanding how to adjust reading rate to purpose. • Use different texts and have students estimate how long it will take to read the text based on purpose for reading and background for the text.
2. Self-Ccorrectors	OK with self-corrections	Slow	Below standard	These students are overly concerned about saying the words correctly and need help focusing on the bigger picture.	• Use independent-level books to help readers acquire a store of sight words. Also use repetitive text as means of building reading vocabulary. Focus on comprehension to emphasize the importance of understanding.
3. Decoders	OK Great effort	Slow	Below standard	These students rely too much on sounding out words.	• Teach students additional word-identification strategies such as using context and recognizing words on sight. • Remind students that reading is about constructing meaning not just sounding out each word. • Check understanding during reading to help the student remember that making meaning is the major purpose for reading.

					Recommendations
4. Word Callers	OK	OK	Below standard	These students can call words with ease; they need help making meaning to understand what is read.	• Have students stop and process what is being read along the way. Ask students to summarize what was read and predict what will happen next. • Allow students to stop and draw a picture about story events. • Provide students with simple organizers that help them keep track of important events in a story or information in a nonfiction text.
5. Word Stumblers	Several errors	OK	Below standard	These students can benefit from being able to recover specific information to complement a general understanding of what is occurring in the story.	• Look at the student's miscues to see if you can spot a pattern about the type of word work that would strengthen the student's reading. This might also help increase initial word accuracy. • Remind students that reading for understanding is the most important goal.
6. Struggling Readers	Difficulty	Slow	Below standard	These students had trouble with all three aspects of reading. They might offer the greatest challenge, but keep in mind that this group included less than 10 percent of the students tested. Not all students who have difficulty with state exams should be seen as disabled.	These students may benefit the most from additional instructional support, time, or alternative methods. They may need the most intensive interventions.

Figure 1–4 *Reader Affect Profiles*

Profile	Description
1. "I hate reading!"	Students who hate reading and will do anything to avoid it. They no longer see themselves as readers.
2. "I don't like reading!"	Differing only in their intensity from the first group, these students dislike reading and will do almost anything to avoid it. They too no longer see themselves as readers and see little value for the reading instruction that might help them.
3. "I'm not very good at reading."	Students who say that they do not read because they are not very good at reading.
4. "Reading is not very important to me."	Students who do not struggle with reading, but reading is a low priority to them. They would rather be doing other activities. They often score high on the social dimension of motivation. They like to interact with others.
5. "I like reading competitions if I can win."	Students who are often motivated by competition but are only motivated if they know they have a chance to win. If not, the motivation disappears quickly.
6. "My teacher says reading is important."	Students who often don't cause much trouble because they are often willing to do whatever teachers ask them. They read because teachers have convinced them it is important.
7. "I love reading."	Students who love to read and choose to read beyond the school walls.

(Based on Baker and Wigfield [1999])

Edmunds and Bauserman (2006) showed that children are insightful about their own learning and can inform instruction. As a result of talking with ninety-one fourth-grade students, the researchers reported six categories that motivate children to read. For each category, Edmunds and Bauserman showed the three motivating factors children mentioned most often. We show their categories and factors in Figure 1–5.

To help teachers interpret their results, Edmunds and Bauserman also list five recommendations to motivate students: self-selection, attention to characteristics of books, personal interests, access to books, and active involvement with others.

Figure 1–5 *Six Categories That Motivate Children's Reading and Factors Most Often Mentioned*

Category	Factors
1. Why children read narrative text	1. Personal interests 2. Book characteristics 3. Choice
2. Why children read expository text	1. Knowledge they gain from it 2. Choice 3. Personal interest
3. Why children read in general	1. Book characteristics 2. Knowledge they gain from reading
4. Sources of motivation	1. Family 2. Teachers 3. Themselves
5. Actions of others	1. Buying or giving books as gifts 2. Reading aloud to children 3. Sharing books
6. Book referral sources	1. School library 2. Teachers 3. Family members 4. Peers

(Based on Edmunds and Bauserman [2006])

So how does this relate to differentiated reading instruction? All of these researchers' findings help teachers see that affective knowledge has great potential for variation from one reader to another. Their discoveries suggest the need for a variety of initiatives targeting specific efforts to impact affective demands of different readers. As we noted in *Books and Beyond* (2006), the affective demands of readers are just as complex as the cognitive demands and that to think otherwise defies conventional wisdom.

In sum, whether we are addressing readers' local, global, and/or affective knowledge, it is quite clear that one size rarely fits all. In fact, we agree with Allington's idea that in an era of scientifically based research there is nothing as antiscientific as a one-size-fits-all mentality when it comes to a literacy program. Let's face it: Any approach has strengths and weaknesses. The exclusive use of any one approach magnifies its weaknesses. The exclusive use of an approach will privilege some readers but not all. Single approaches fail to account for changes in readers over time or in different contexts. Mandating single approaches disarms teachers from being adequately equipped to help all children who happen to be their responsibility in any given school year. Extremes rarely work.

Belief #3: Differentiation Must Address Contemporary Classroom Demands

Given that all children are and will continue to be different, teachers will always need some kind of differentiated instruction to address these differences, regardless of whether it is a "hot topic." The current reauthorization of IDEA passed by Congress in 2004 attempts to catch reading problems as early as possible thereby shrinking the number of students who might otherwise be referred to special education for additional services. Response to Intervention is a vehicle for carrying out this legislation, and, we believe, is the catalyst for making differentiated instruction a "hot topic" once again.

Despite the way it is sometimes interpreted, Response to Intervention (or, RTI) is anything but a single, specific approach to teaching reading and therefore certainly fits with the underlying assumptions about differentiated reading instruction. It is a process of implementing high-quality, scientifically researched instruction; monitoring student progress; and adjusting instruction based on student response (NASDE and CASE 2006). The goal of RTI is to expand the range and diversity of prevention and intervention options to enhance outcomes for all students. Ultimately, RTI is designed to ensure that labeling and referral are the last resort for students with special needs.

Basically, RTI is a three-step process that begins with providing all children with the best possible instruction and taking a look at how they perform. This first round of instruction (i.e., Tier 1) usually occurs in the classroom context and the classroom teacher provides the instruction. The goal of Tier 1 is to enhance success and reduce barriers to learning for as many students as possible. This level requires that an initial effort is made to make sure that all children benefit from the highest-quality classroom instruction. Even when that instruction takes place in whole-class arrangements, efforts must be made to target specific students. Effective classroom instruction is usually the most efficient use of time and resources to help students with their needs.

If some children make little or no progress when compared to their peers in the regular classroom instruction, they are provided with a second round of instruction (i.e., Tier 2). No matter how good classroom instruction may be, it can be a challenge to ensure that all students' needs are met.

The teacher needs to think about how to add a layer of additional intervention that targets individuals even further. How do teachers provide help to students who need a little more time beyond what can be offered during regular classroom instruction? Tier 2 initiatives are identified as *selected options*. These may include the teacher and/or another professional, such as a reading teacher or a special education teacher, providing supplementary instruction. It may take place within the classroom or outside of the classroom. Small-group configurations can allow different professionals to work with different groups and therefore provide more direct support for students who need it. Individual professionals could also carve out time to work with a fewer number of students targeting outcomes with which they need help. These efforts require more demands on instructional time and resources, but still offer a more efficient attempt to help students in need than referring them to special programs.

If the children still make little progress, additional assessment is often administered to identify specific problem areas. Children are then provided with a third round of intensive instruction (i.e., Tier 3). This is in addition to the efforts made in Tier 1 and 2 initiatives. Tier 3 efforts are often called *targeted options*. Few students need these options. They include specifically designed and customized instructional approaches that fit the individual. The options are intended for students who have a high likelihood of developing a lasting pattern of academic failure or high level of social or emotional distress. This level starts to place greater demands in terms of time and resources on the teacher.

As you can see, RTI is about designing and delivering the best possible literacy instruction and paying attention to how children perform. The goal is to continually discover what children know and need to know in order to help them advance as readers. It serves as a good reminder that *readers differ*. Allington and Walmsley (2007) remind us that, "what's most important is that struggling students are offered targeted, expert, and intensive reading instruction before they are labeled as students with disabilities" (ix). RTI also leads us right back to the importance of a knowledgeable teacher. Clearly, *teachers matter!* Allington and Walmsey explain that "[t]he success of any RTI initiative will rest largely on the ability of the teachers to select appropriate instructional activities based on the diagnostic evidence each students provides at the onset and throughout the intervention" (x).

Allington and Walmsey caution teachers to be careful in seeing RTI as the quick fix to all our problems. In fact, they suggest that it might be nothing more than "old wine with a new label" (vii). And despite RTI's emergence during an era of strong federal mandates and scientifically based, they point out that there is no legal requirement to use a three-tier model and no research to prove that a Tier 3 model is effective. They conclude, "There are many RTI models and the regulations are written to accommodate the many different models that are currently in use."

Looking beyond the horizon, RTI might not be the last stop as federal policies push schools toward differentiation models. Some legislators are now promoting a "universal design for learning" educational framework. It relies on three principles to guide teachers as they use technology and other means to reach students with different learning styles, such as those with disabilities or learning English:

- Provide multiple, flexible methods of presentation that give students various ways to acquire information

- Provide multiple, flexible methods of expression that offer students alternatives for demonstrating what they know

- Provide multiple, flexible options for engagement to help students get interested, be challenged, and stay motivated

These principles certainly reflect our differentiated instruction views. We believe they are certainly keys to successful instruction. But it will be very interesting to observe what might occur if they suddenly become mandated as a result of future federal policy!

Belief #4: Differentiated Instruction Needs to Address the Needs of English Language Learners

English language learners (ELLs) are those children whose native languages are not English. Nonetheless, there are several terms that are often used when talking about children who speak languages other than English. These include English as a second language (ESL), English as a foreign language (EFL), limited English proficient (LEP), English for speakers of other languages (ESOL), and bilingual (i.e., use of two languages). Like Freeman and Freeman (2007), we use the term *ELL* because it is more accurate. That is, in some cases, English might be their third or fourth language! So they really are English language learners.

As we talk about differentiated instruction, then, we need to remember that while ELLs are often treated as a separate group, we need to use caution in treating all students within that group as the same. Different language systems bring different problem-solving challenges for learners. Imagine teaching concepts of print to a child who knows Arabic or the trickiness of alphabet letters to a child who uses a character-based language. How does a teacher teach ELLs in a culturally relevant style using texts from different cultures when the students may represent as many cultures as languages? In addition to these instructional challenges, new research is emerging to suggest that different categories of ELLs may benefit differently from some times of instruction. For example, McKeown and Gentilucci (2007) discovered that strong metacognitive strategy instruction was most effective with less advanced ELLs, but was less effective with initial ELLs and actually detrimental to advanced ELLs.

In the end, it is the student's level of English proficiency that often determines the learner's instructional needs. Fortunately, there are some sources that help teachers to better understand these proficiency levels and how to differentiate their instruction accordingly. One such reference is *Strategies and Resources for Mainstream Teachers of English Language Learners* (Reed and Railsbeck 2003). This resource lays out English Language Proficiency levels with accompanying descriptions, student behaviors one might expect to see at these different levels, and some ways to use oral language to prompt or cue students. All of this information is shown in Figure 1–6.

Building on this knowledge, Figure 1–7 goes one step further by providing some specific ideas for how teachers can differentiate instruction so that they attend not only to ELLs as a group, but across the group. And, as you will discover, many of these ideas show themselves in the grouping structures and the sample lessons provided in Chapters 3 through 6.

Putting all of this information together brings you to our big idea. As with any children you encounter, ELLs have strengths and needs and, just like with all other students, we need to determine what these needs are so that we can better help them advance in their ability to acquire English while at the same time valuing their other language(s). ELLs bring much with them, just like all students.

Belief #5: Teachers Matter

What we know about how readers differ highlights the importance of knowledgeable teachers who are able to make decisions with their particular students in mind. But just what do we mean by being knowledgeable? We believe that knowledgeable teachers are those who understand the content of reading, have the ability to plan and organize instruction, know about and call on several different instructional strategies, have high yet realistic expectations for all learners, and have a positive attitude toward children; they tend to see

Figure 1–6 *English Language Proficiency Levels with Expectations and Questions or Cues*

Level and Description	Expect	Oral Language Prompts/Cues
Level 1—Preproduction/Entering (lasts 10 hours–6 mos.) • Student does not understand or speak English with the exception of a few isolated words or expressions.	• Head nodding, pointing, or physically demonstrating • A silent period • May understand, but not use, five hundred receptive words	• "Show me . . ." • "Which of these . . . ?" • "Point to . . ." • "Is this a . . . ?"
Level 2—Early Production/Beginning (lasts approx. 6 mos.) • Student understands and speaks conversational and academic English with hesitancy and difficulty. • Student understands parts of lessons and simple directions. • Student is at a preemergent level of reading and writing in English, significantly below grade level.	• Expect one- or two-word responses, making choices from simple language samples • May understand and use one thousand receptive/active words	• Yes or no questions • "Is it the _____ one or the _____ one?" • Use *who, what, when,* or *where* prompts
Level 3—Intermediate/Developing (lasts approx. 1 year) • Student understands and speaks conversational and academic English with decreasing hesitancy and difficulty. • Student is postemergent, developing reading comprehension and writing skills in English. • Student's English literacy skills allow the student (with assistance) to demonstrate academic knowledge in content areas.	• Expect phrases or short sentences with some grammatical errors • May have three thousand words	• "What happened first, next . . . ?" • "Tell me about . . ." • "Describe . . ."

Level 4—Advanced Intermediate/Expanding/Intermediate Fluency (lasts approx. 1 year) • Student understands and speaks conversational English without apparent difficulty, but understands and speaks academic English with some hesitancy. • Student continues to acquire reading and writing skills in content areas to achieve grade-level expectations (with assistance).	• Expect longer sentences and fewer grammatical errors • May have approximately six thousand words	• "What was the character trying to do?" • "What is your opinion?" • "How are _____ and _____ similar/different?"
Level 5—Advanced/Bridging (may take 5 to 7 years to achieve) • Student understands and speaks conversational and academic English well. • Student is near proficient in reading, writing, and content-area skills needed to meet grade-level expectations. • Student requires occasional support.	• Expect the student to be able to understand and speak conversational and academic English very near to grade level with occasional support • Specialized content vocabulary	• Teaching techniques and assessment used with most of the English-speaking students • Provide support as needed
Level 6—Formerly Limited English Proficient/Now Fully English Proficient (Searching) • Student was formerly limited English proficient and is now fully English proficient. • Student reads, writes, speaks, and comprehends English within academic classroom settings.	• Expect average and above performance	

Figure 1–7 *Ways to Differentiate for ELLs*

Silent/Receptive Level 1	Early Production Level 2	Speech Emergence Level 3	Intermediate/Advanced Proficiency Levels 4 and 5
Use of visual aids and gestures	Engage students in charades and linguistic guessing games	Conduct group discussions	Sponsor student panel discussions on the thematic topics
Slow speech emphasizing key words	Do role-playing activities	Use skits for dramatic interaction	Have students identify a social issue and defend their position
Do not force oral production	Present open-ended sentences	Have student fill out forms and application	Promote critical analysis and evaluation of pertinent issues
Write key words on the board with students copying them as they are presented	Promote open dialogues	Assign writing compositions	Assign writing tasks that involve writing, rewriting, editing, and critiquing written examples
Use pictures and manipulatives to help illustrate concepts	Conduct student interviews with the guidelines written out	Have students write descriptions of visuals and props	Encourage critical interpretation of stories, legends, and poetry
Use multimedia language role models	Use charts, tables, graphs, and other conceptual visuals	Use music, TV, and radio, with class activities	Have students design questions, directions, and activities for others to follow
Use interactive dialogue journals	Use newspaper ads and other mainstream materials to encourage language interaction	Show films and videos with cooperative groups scripting the visuals	Encourage appropriate age storytelling
Encourage choral readings	Encourage partner and trio readings	Encourage solo readings with interactive comprehension checks	
Use Total Physical Response (TPR) techniques			

them half full rather than half empty. These teachers use all of what they know about instruction and an array of materials, including many different kinds of texts, to stimulate and advance children's growth.

Our list of characteristics is in keeping with findings of classroom-based research (e.g., Wharton-McDonald, Pressley, and Hampston 1999; Taylor, Pearson, Clark, and Walpole 2000; Allington and Johnson 2002). If we turn to the research on exemplary teachers (Wharton-McDonald, Pressley, and Hampston 1999), we can identify practices and beliefs of teachers who, when given students of similar demographics, were able to produce greater student results on measures of performance and achievement. These high-impact, exemplary teachers shared eight common characteristics:

1. Coherent and thorough integration of skills with high-quality reading and writing experiences

2. A high density of instruction (i.e., integration of multiple goals in a single lesson)

3. Extensive use of scaffolding (i.e., support)

4. Encouragement of student self-regulation (i.e., helping students solve their own problems)

5. A thorough integration of reading and writing activities

6. High expectations for all students

7. Masterful classroom management

8. An awareness of their practices and goals underlying them

While all eight of these characteristics may be important, two may be especially critical in providing differentiated instruction. Clearly, a teacher who provides dense instruction by addressing multiple goals for different students in the same lesson is more able to differentiate instruction. Likewise, a teacher who is masterful at scaffolding is more able to differentiate instruction. Knowing where students are at, knowing where students need to be, and being able to provide a bridge between those points is also a key for effectively differentiating instruction.

Add to these findings Allington and Johnson's (2002) finding that in the most effective fourth-grade classrooms instruction took place in a variety of formats (i.e., whole class, different types of small groups) and you have yet another research-based reason for using the different grouping structures we propose in this book. Given that students are more likely to excel when they engage in a variety of grouping structures leaves us with little choice. We need to know and use different grouping structures to better ensure students' reading growth.

Without a doubt, research findings like these help to validate what we as teachers already know: Teaching is a complex behavior that requires us to perform many different roles in order to reach as many readers as possible. We need to know how to plan differentiated instruction, organize all of the students so that they feel safe and secure enough to take the necessary risks that accompany learning, and we need to be able to evaluate ourselves, to reflect on why we do what we do and if what we are doing is working with the children we are fortunate to teach.

Conclusion

Grounded with a better understanding of how readers differ and teachers matter leaves you better equipped to explore the remainder of this text. Regardless of the grouping model you choose to begin with, our bottom line is that all children can read age-appropriate texts if they are provided with the support they need for that text. And, as you now know, because readers differ, they will need different levels and kinds of support. The four grouping models we explain are a means for helping you provide these different levels of support thereby making reading an enjoyable and successful experience for all readers, no matter how different they might be.

Grouping Structures Overview

Musicians seated, instruments tuned to the first violin, the orchestra readies itself for the conductor's entrance. The conductor walks onto the stage and, after taking the necessary bows, steps onto the conducting platform facing the orchestra. As he raises his arms, baton in his right hand, musicians poise their instruments to begin playing the first part of the musical score. Arms held high, baton in hand, the conductor moves both arms to signal the musicians to play. Throughout the music, the conductor uses the musical score as a guide to make sure the music is performed as intended by the composer, which necessitates a variety of gestures. Some of the conductor's gestures convey to the musicians to join in so that all are playing together. At other times, he signals some musicians to play and for others to remain silent. At still other times, he motions to a single musician to play a section of the musical score solo.

What's going on here has as much to do with differentiating instruction and using different grouping structures to teach reading as it does playing a musical score! Like the conductor, teachers use a plan to help them know when to work with students as a whole group, when to work with smaller groups within the whole, and when to have students work independently. And like the conductor, teachers use these different grouping options to help us accomplish a given purpose. In other words, rather than relying on one grouping technique to the exclusion of the others, teachers use a combination knowing that each group size has advantages and disadvantages (see Figure 2–1) and that there are optimal conditions when each works best. Our understanding replaces an *either/or* mind-set.

The four grouping models we propose in Chapters 3 to 6 capitalize on our understanding of how to best use a variety of grouping structures, often

Figure 2–1 *Planning for Different Group Sizes*

Group Size	Description	Advantages	Disadvantages	When It Works
Whole Class	• Teacher works with the whole class and everyone participates in similar activities. In one way or another, the same text is often read by all students.	• Builds a community of learners. • Provides a common knowledge base for all.	• Differentiating instruction is more difficult. • Some students can get frustrated or bored depending on the level of instruction. • Students may not interact as planned.	• Different learners are considered when planning instruction. • All members of the class are provided with a similar experience.
Small Group	• Groups of two to five students work together to accomplish a given task.	• Provides for focused instruction. • Engages more learners. • Students learn to work with one another.	• Students may not interact. • Creates a higher noise level. • Students might be grouped together for too long. • Student perceptions of group can be negative.	• Group membership changes on a regular basis. • Students are taught how to respond to one another.
Partners	• Students are paired up with one another to read text in one or more ways.	• Stays focused. • Enables relationships to develop. • Encourages independent learning so the teacher can help those who need it.	• One of the two students may become too dependent on the other. • One of the two may dominate.	• Partners are switched on a regular basis. • Procedures are clearly understood by both.
Individual	• Students work by themselves and each often reads a different text.	• Allows students to read at a comfortable level and to develop their own understandings. • Enables teacher to evaluate individual progress to determine what students know and need to know.	• Can be hard to organize. • Students may become distracted and/or lose focus. • Little sense of community.	• Reading is at the appropriate level. • Students understand procedures. • An effort is made to bring students back together either as a small group or large group to discuss what they've learned.

(Opitz and Ford 2000)

within one lesson, as a means for differentiating instruction. Just like four different musical scores cause a conductor to use different sections of the orchestra at specific times to accomplish different purposes throughout the piece, so, too, the grouping models cause us to use different sections of the class at specific times to accomplish specific reading support purposes. Figure 2–2 provides an overview of these grouping models and how each highlights differentiation.

As Figure 2–2 shows, there are differences in how differentiation plays out among the different grouping structures. Nonetheless, they are similar in seven ways.

1. *A variety of group sizes are used within any given reading lesson.* Every reading lesson begins with calling the class together as a whole group for a focus lesson. Students then break out into a smaller group and read and respond to a text independent of other groups. Students then come back to the large group to conclude the reading experience.

2. *The lesson structure contains the same three elements: frontloading, reading and responding, and extending.* As a way to set students up for reading success, the lesson begins by providing or accessing students' backgrounds and providing demonstrations and/or explanations so that students will know exactly what it is they need to accomplish. All are then provided time to read and respond. The reading session then concludes with an inclusive whole-group activity. Each of these three lesson elements carries some important reminders. We list these in Figure 2–4.

3. *There is a deliberate effort to use a variety of teaching and learning strategies.* Recognizing that readers not only differ in their reading preferences and profiles but also in their learning styles, the structures enable the teacher to use visuals for those who need them, oral directions for those who lean toward learning through listening, and hands-on activities for those learners who are both kinesthetic and tactile. Likewise, a variety of ways of responding to text enables students to choose the mode of expression that will best help show their understanding. Some students might want to draw a response to text whereas others prefer to write in one form or another.

Figure 2–2 *Grouping Models and How They Highlight Differentiation*

Grouping Structure	Brief Description	Chapter	Differentiation Highlights
Grouping Without Tracking	Whole-class approach in which the teacher provides different levels of support for students reading and responding to a common core text.	3	• Varying amounts of support are provided to enable all readers to engage with the text. Some groups read independently whereas others read with the teacher. Still others listen to the teacher read aloud as they follow along. • Reaches readers who fit the *Reader Affective Profile 3* (see Figure 1–4) because text is selected and frontloaded to help students gain greater confidence in reading.
Jigsawing	Small-group approach in which similar achievement groups are formed to read and respond to different parts of a whole-class text. The text is intentionally divided so that parts vary in their degree of challenge.	4	• Repetitive reading to enable students to practice a chunk of text. • Accessible grade-level content by breaking up the text into manageable chunks for all readers and assigning different chunks to different readers depending on their reading level. • Reaches readers who fit *Reader Affective Profiles 1, 2,* or *3* because the text is shorter making it more likely that students will be able to successfully read the text in a short amount of time.
Connected Literature Circles	Small-group approach in which similar achievement groups are formed to read and respond to different texts of varying degrees of challenge that are related by topic, theme, genre, author, and/or strategy.	5	• Multiple copies of different texts are used for different groups of students who are of similar reading achievement. • Reaches readers who fit *Reader Affective Profile 4* because of the social aspect that coincides with literature circles.
Focused Readers' Workshop	Individualized approach in which all readers read and respond to different but related texts. Again, texts may be linked by topic, theme, genre, author, and/or strategy. Individualized texts may come from a collection of resources with varying degrees of challenge.	6	• Readers read at their pace. There is no need to have all students finish a given book within a given time segment. • Individualized in that all readers are reading different texts that relate to a common theme. • Individual conferences with the teacher enable the teacher to monitor and adjust instruction for future lessons. • Reaches readers who fit all *Reader Affective Profiles* because students are provided time to self-select a just-right text of interest. It is especially effective for reaching readers with *Reader Affective Profiles 1* or *2,* however, because students get to use their interests as a way to select a text. They are more motivated to read their self-selected text and to start to see themselves as readers.

4. *All enable children to read by reading.* Regardless of the structure, all children, regardless of perceived reading level, read appropriate texts. They learn to read as much or more by reading as they do when being taught about reading. Successful differentiation requires careful attention to text selection. Careful text selection, however, means considering factors beyond an identified level for the book.

5. *Varying the degree of teacher support is a critical tool for differentiation.* While students are reading and responding, the teacher provides varying levels of support to better ensure reading success. Instead of altering the tasks or lowering expectations, the teacher analyzes the level of support needed by different students. The teacher provides varying degrees of direct or indirect support based on students' needs.

6. *Open-ended activities enable all children to participate.* All readers can complete the response activities at their own level because the activities are designed such that they can. For example, all children keep a literature response log and respond to their reading in one or more ways. When responding in writing, their writing is representative of where each is functioning.

7. *All are based on our beliefs about differentiated instruction.* Recognizing that knowing why we do what we do yields high student achievement (Pressley 2005), we set forth our beliefs in Chapter 1 (see pages 1–22).

So there you have it; an overview of the four grouping structures we showcase in Chapters 3 through 6. But before we bring this chapter to a close, there are four additional points we need to emphasize.

First, let's remember that successful differentiated instruction begins with knowledge of literacy demands and the students we are teaching. This elevates the role of assessment as a driving force in differentiating instruction. We need to know what is critical for becoming successful readers and writers and how to assess those elements. Since assessment has been a focus of our work in the past (Opitz and Ford 2000), we will refer you to that resource to explore issues related to assessing learners. The primary reason for assessing is to inform our thinking and influence our planning. (See Figure 2–3.)

Figure 2–3 *Instructional Cycle Informed by Assessment*

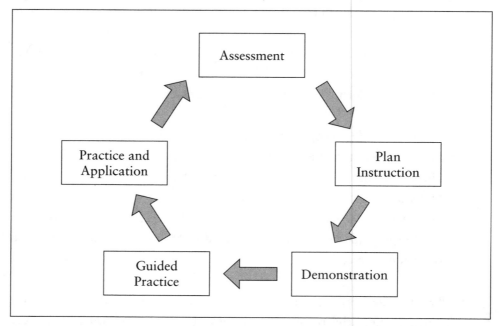

Assessment will lead you to the following key questions:

■ What do assessment results tell me about each of my students?

■ Which target skills and strategies can I identify?

■ Which of my students need to work together as a group at this time?

■ How much time is required per group?

■ What resources are available for me?

■ How do I organize the classroom during the reading block in order to manage differentiated instruction?

It's the last question that brings us to our second reminder. In selecting which model to use in organizing your differentiated instruction, there are several considerations to keep in mind as you prepare to use the three-part lesson plan that is common to all four models. We show these in Figure 2–4.

Third, in keeping with our earlier writing about grouping, we deliberately use the terms *similar achievement* in place of *homogeneous* and *mixed achievement* in place of *heterogeneous* when we discuss grouping in each model. We do so because we believe, as do others (e.g., Allington and

Figure 2–4 *Reminders for the Three-Part Lesson Plan Common to All Grouping Models*

Lesson Component	Reminders
Frontloading	• Time invested on the front end of the lesson guarantees that more students will be better able to work independently from you thereby reducing the number of students who will need support. • Gradually turn over the responsibility for the reading of and responding to the text to the students by moving from modeling to guided practice to independent practice. This will also ensure that more students will be able to work successfully away from you. • Make sure the purpose and directions for independent reading and writing are clear for all students before turning over the activity to students and starting any instruction with a small group or individual in need of more support.
Reading and Responding	• Engagement activities should be developed so that they encourage students or teams to actually read the assigned texts or parts of texts. Assist them in processing the texts and create a paper trail that can be used when responding to the text. The paper trail also can provide information for quick assessments of students' reading performance and independent work skills. • Hold the same expectations for all students and then differentiate the level of support and/or texts during reading and responding. • Discourage the use of activities within small groups in reading and responding to the text that promotes disengagement (e.g., round-robin reading). Make sure students have seen and practiced many meaningful alternatives. • Allow for some choice in how students can respond their reading.
Extending	• Activities should allow all students to contribute to the follow-up activity in mixed achievement groups. Activities should allow all members of a team to play a role in sharing what was learned with others. • Activity should allow students to build on instruction provided during the frontloading and practiced during the reading. • The activity should allow teams, partners, or individuals to use this text as a springboard for additional inquiry. • Encourage teams or individuals to reflect on their work together to improve team and independent work skills throughout the year.

(Adapted from Ford [2005a])

Cunningham 1996), that tapping innate ability is difficult if not impossible. The only conclusion that can be drawn from how children perform on different reading measurements is just that: we assess their performance rather than their potential ability. Therefore, talking about achievement is much more accurate than talking about ability. No two children are alike and to assume otherwise is faulty thinking. We take to heart what Betts noted years ago: "When groupings are made for any activity, the teacher should not assume that homogeneity is assured. In fact, homogeneity is a fiction" (1946, 391).

As you can see by reading this quotation, we are not the first, nor are we alone when we exclaim *readers differ!*

The fourth and final reminder is that some musical scores are more complex than others and conductors who know their orchestra members choose the score accordingly. The conductor then gradually selects more complex scores so that all can meet with success while at the same time grow as musicians. The same can be said for these grouping models. The first is easier to orchestrate than the fourth. One way to scaffold your learning right along with your students is to choose the model that will afford all with just-right growth, adjusting as needed. Like orchestral conductors, *teachers matter!*

Model 1:
Grouping Without Tracking

Model 1
Grouping Without Tracking
Same Text for All Students
Differentiating and Targeting Through Levels of Support

Frontloading
All students involved in a variety of activities in a large group, mixed small groups, pairs, and individually.

Students Who Need Support to Read and Respond
Teachers work directly with similar achievement small group in need of support.

Students Who Can Read and Respond Independently
Students are engaged in reading and responding to text more independently; indirectly guided by the structures created by the teacher.

Follow Up
Bring all students together to demonstrate understanding through response in a large group, mixed small groups, pairs, and individually.

Figure 3–1

Scenario

You recognize that one way for students to read grade-level material is to give them the opportunity to read grade-level content. You are not fooled, however. You know that your students are very diverse. Your observations and your students' performance on reading-related tasks and on mandated tests have shown you that your students are reading at many different reading levels. Therefore, you know that some students will need more support when reading grade-level content if they are to be successful and truly learn something from the reading experience. Others will be able to read the text independently. This information about your students and the text you want them to read leads you to use the grouping without tracking model for planning successful reading experiences.

Explanation

Grouping without tracking as we define and describe it in this chapter was designed by Jean Paratore (1990) to assist teachers in more effectively addressing the diverse needs of learners in a classroom when using the same text with all students. There are two major tenets that set this grouping without tracking model apart from other grouping structures. First, all students are held to the same high expectations. Using this model, the teacher keeps all of the students together at the start of the lesson, varies the amount of support provided during the reading and responding sections of the lesson, and pulls the class together at the end of the lesson to share common understandings. In this way, then, all students have access to the same quality instruction, authentic children's literature included. Second, because the answer to the question of which students can independently read and respond to the text will vary across time, texts, and contexts, different students will need more or less support depending on the task at hand. Consequently, those requiring the teacher's support will vary. No student can or should remain stuck in the same group for an extended period of time.

As we show in Figure 3–1, during the first part of this model, the teacher keeps all students together in an intensive prereading phase that frontloads the lesson with teaching strategies designed to level the playing field for all students, which ensures that all students experience reading success.

The teacher then differentiates the level of support that students receive when they read and respond to the text. The answer to the critical question, "Which of my students can read and respond to the text on their own?," enables the teacher to set up an infrastructure that allows those students who can independently read and respond with little or no teacher support to do just that. For those students in need of more help, the teacher provides assistance by reading and responding with them in a small-group setting while the remaining students read independently.

One last defining feature of the grouping without tracking model is the extending part of the lesson. During this part of the model, the teacher brings all students back together to extend their reading and responding. In this way, students contribute to the learning of others, as a classroom community. Figure 3–2 shows the key elements of grouping without tracking model and a brief explanation of each element.

Figure 3–2 *Key Elements of the Grouping Without Tracking Model*

Key Elements	Grouping Without Tracking Model
Text	Use the same text for all students. Use the same selection from a basal anthology or textbook or a children's literature selection such as Patricia Reilly Giff's *Nory Ryan's Song* (Aladdin, 2000).
Grouping	Use whole-class grouping for the frontloading and extending parts of the lesson and small groups, partners, and independent reading for the reading and responding part of the lesson.
Differentiation	Provide different levels of support to students as they read and respond to text; some students will get direct support whereas others will be indirectly guided by engagement structures set up for independent reading and responding while away from the teacher.
Best Uses	Use this model when the same text needs to be experienced by all learners in the classroom community such as common trade books, basal anthology selections, and/or content-area textbook selections used as springboards for additional study.
Advantages	• It builds community across the classroom by providing shared experiences. • It is an efficient use of time and materials. • It allows the teacher to provide support to those students who need it while others are kept engaged with similar tasks. • It accelerates students' progress—especially for those who struggle with reading—because they are exposed to grade-level content, which broadens their global knowledge base, while being provided teacher-mediated instruction.
Disadvantages	• Students who worked with the teacher must be given time to read independently or with minimal support away from the teacher. • Students who worked away from the teacher will need an opportunity to meet with the teacher to scaffold learning with texts beyond those used in community activity.

General Teaching Suggestions

Preparation

1. Select a text that most students can read and respond to independently and one that the remaining students would be able to read and respond to if provided direct support from the teacher.

2. Plan prereading activities that will adequately frontload the lesson for all readers. Focus on standards-based skills and strategies that students need as revealed in ongoing assessments.

3. Plan response activities that will engage as many students as possible to work independently away from the teacher. If possible, let these flow from the instruction done in the prereading phase of the lesson.

4. Be prepared to directly provide support and additional instruction to those students who will require additional teacher guidance.

5. Plan extension activities that bring the class together as a community of learners and in which all students can make an important contribution. If possible, let these activities build on the frontloading and engagement activities.

Frontloading

1. Activate schema about the text. Get all students thinking about the topic or theme.

2. Develop needed background knowledge for the text.

3. Address any skills, strategies, and vocabulary needed to successfully read the text.

4. Generate interest about the text.

5. Read aloud a short selection from the beginning of the text. Use think-alouds to model how to do the response activity. As appropriate, have the students replicate your work as you model.

6. To provide guided practice, invite all students to read the next selection of the text with you using choral reading or an informal readers' theatre. As the students are reading with you, prompt the students to tell you how to add to the response activity. As appropriate, have students add to their work with you.

7. To provide independent practice, invite all students to read one more selection of the text on their own while in the large group. Focus their reading and follow up to see that the purpose for reading was accomplished. As they are reading on their own, monitor and probe to see that they can add to the response activity without you.

8. Set a clear purpose for reading and responding to the rest of the text.

9. Provide visible written directions for independent work.

Reading and Responding

1. Turn the completion of the task modeled and practiced during the frontloading over to those students who you believe can read and respond to the text on their own.

   - Review the directions as needed.

   - Review any class rules about reading and responding independently as needed.

   - Clearly identify one or two activities that the students can do when they are finished reading and responding, if you are still working with your small group.

   - Monitor the students as they start on the reading and response activity.

2. Once the students are independently reading and responding, call together those students in need of additional support and provide them with appropriate instruction. This instruction might include any of the following:

   - Review any of the frontloading activities as needed.

   - Address any other critical skills more appropriate for this group.

   - Assist them in the reading of the text. Depending on the length of the text and the ability of the students, you may choose to read the text aloud to them, read the text together, read with partners, paraphrase certain sections, or use any combination of techniques.

   - Be intentional about identifying at least part of the text the students could read on their own orally or silently.

   - Provide support in completing the response activity including additional modeling and guided practice as needed.

- Be intentional about identifying at least part of the response activity that the students would complete on their own.

- Monitor students to assess understanding and work habits.

Extending

1. All students should be able to contribute to the postreading activity. In developing postreading project work, use this as an opportunity to set up mixed achievement groups.

2. Review the written responses by those students who read and responded independently to assess level of engagement and understanding. Adjust group membership next time based on information you collect by reviewing students' written responses during small-group time.

3. Provide additional time for the students in the support group to read texts independently at their instructional level.

4. Provide additional opportunities for students who independently read and responded to meet with you for interaction around additional texts they are reading.

Illustration of a Primary Lesson

As part of a larger unit on folktales, Josh wants his third graders to read *Bringing the Rain to Kapiti Plain* (Aardema 1981), a folktale that is in the basal anthology. It is a fitting example of a folktale while at the same time serves as a perfect segue into learning more about Africa, which they have started learning about in social studies. This particular folktale will help students learn more about landforms and geographical locations because both are highlighted. He will also use the folktale to teach students more about how to read with prosodic features of language (i.e., phrasing, expression, intonation) so that students better understand how these features can further their enjoyment of reading and comprehending the author's intended meaning. Finally, Josh is excited about showing his students the paperback version of this story. It just so happens that the publishers of the basal anthology he is required to use included the very same version in the anthology, illustrations and all. What he will point out to his students is that they can find this book in bookstores and the library should they want to have a copy of it for further reading.

When looking at this folktale, Josh realizes that the language features will enable most students to read it with ease. The author uses rhyme, rhythm, and repetition throughout the book. What's more is that a cumulative pattern is used to construct the folktale, which is really more like a lyrical poem. Still, there will be some students who will feel overwhelmed with the text as a whole. Without realizing that specific language features are used that will facilitate their reading, at a glance, these students are likely to shut down when they see how many words appear on a page. His students in mind, then, Josh uses the grouping without tracking model to plan his lesson. (See Figure 3–3 for his completed plan and Appendix B for a blank Grouping Without Tracking Lesson Plan form.)

Frontloading

Josh opens the lesson by having students recall what they have been learning about geographical features of some countries and how the map indicates these features. He comments, "We have been learning that there are many different landforms and the people who create maps use colors to signal these different land forms." He then reminds students what they have been learning about folktales stating, "You have also been learning about the different characteristics that make up a folktale. Like the creators of maps, the authors of these folktales give you some clues to let you know that the story is indeed a folktale. However, sometimes not all of these elements are included. Take a look at our class grid as a reminder." Josh points to the chart that shows the folktale characteristics. (See Figure 3–4.) He continues, "Today we are going to connect what you know about geographical landforms and folktales. You are going to be reading a folktale that originated in Africa. Let's take a look at Africa on the map." He asks all students to look at the map and find Africa. He calls on a volunteer to show the rest of the class and asks the rest of the class to raise their hand if they agree. He then says, "Now that we have located it,

> *Notice Josh's use of the world map and the class grid thereby attending to the needs of learners in both methods of presentation and options for engagement. Simply orally referencing the map and grid, Josh knows, will not be effective to meet the various needs of learners.*

> *Take note of Josh's use of pairing with a neighbor to identify and express background knowledge. This attention to providing flexible options for engagement will help students remain focused throughout his lesson while capitalizing on some students' strengths in interpersonal and verbal skills.*

Figure 3–3 *Josh's Grouping Without Tracking Lesson Plan*

Content Area: Language Arts (reading) and Social Studies (geography) **Content Objective:** To identify elements of folktales; to identify landforms mentioned in the folktale. **Comprehension and Fluency Objective:** To enhance the understanding of text by using prosodic features of language (i.e., phrasing, intonation, and expression).	
Text(s)	*Bringing the Rain to Kapiti Plain* (Verna Aardema 1981). New York: Scholastic. ISBN: 0590428705.
Frontloading (Before Reading) • **Whole Class**	1. Remind children what they have been learning about in geography: Different geographical locations have different topographical features. 2. Remind students about the elements of folktales by referring to the characteristics shown on the grid and that the folktales they will be reading today may have some or all of these characteristics (refer to Figure 3–4). 3. Tell students that the folktale they will be reading is a Nandi Tale from Africa. Use the world map to show where Africa is located and discuss topographical features and what signals them on a map. 4. Have all students turn to the table of contents in their basal anthology to locate the title *Bringing the Rain to Kapiti Plain* and what page they should turn to so that they can preview the story. Write the title on the board for those who might need to refer back to it. Circulate and help as needed. 5. Once all of the students have found the story, invite them to do a picture walk. This should only take two minutes. 6. Based on the pictures, have students make predictions about the folktale. Write their ideas on the whiteboard. 7. Introduce words that may pose difficulty by using sentences from the text that contain them and inviting students to record words in box grids: *Kapiti Plain, Ki-Pat, acacia.*
Reading and Responding (During Reading) • **Groups**	1. Provide time for students to independently and silently read the story. 2. Remind students that they can choose to read the additional folktales if they finish reading while you are still reading with a group of students. 3. Once students have started reading, call together those students who need additional support with reading. Read aloud the first part of the story to them and point to the lines that repeat so that students can see firsthand how the story repeats. Once you have modeled the pattern, have them attempt the next part of text on their own by reading silently. Observe and provide help as needed.

Figure 3–3 *Continued*

39

Model 1: Grouping Without Tracking

Extending (After Reading)	*Day 1:* 1. Call students together. 2. Review today's reading and responding. 3. Fill in class folktale grid. 4. Review the topographical features shown in the story. 5. Display the other folktales and provide additional time for students to select those that they can read with ease. *Day 2:* 1. Strategically group students into mixed achievement groups. 2. Give each group a chart that contains one stanza from the folktale and provide time for the students to practice reading it as a group so that they can read it in unison with ease. Use a different color pen to write each stanza. 3. Show the class the remaining charts that you have constructed and written in black. 4. Provide groups with time to practice reading their stanza. 5. Explain to the class that the stanzas are numbered as are the charts and that you will practice reading the story in numerical order. Each group is responsible for reading its chart in turn. However, any time the class sees black print, that is the signal to read as a whole class. 6. After reading the entire story, provide groups with art materials so that they can illustrate their stanza. 7. Reread the story only this time, as the group reads its stanza, one group member displays his or her illustration of it while the rest read. 8. Close the lesson by reminding students that making reading sound like talking is a way to make the reading more enjoyable. It can also help you to convey to the listener the meaning of your story.

take a look at the colors that are used to show the topography of Africa. What kinds of landforms would you expect to see if you visited Africa? Turn to your neighbor and tell them something you know about the land-forms of Africa." After students have had a chance to share with each other, he surfaces a number of responses. Josh states, "The folktale you are going to read today happens on a plain. It's called Kapiti Plain." He writes the words on the board as he speaks. "Turn to your neighbor and whisper what kind of landform you think a plain is. Tell your neighbor what color would probably be used to signal it."

Figure 3–4 *Josh's Folktale Grid*

Folktale Class Matrix					
Characteristics/Title	Repetition is used.	There are characters with magical powers.	A magical transformation occurs.	A magic object is used.	Trickery is used.

Having reviewed landforms, Josh proceeds to the reading of the folktale. He comments, "Turn to the Table of Contents in your anthology and find the title, *Bringing the Rain to Kapiti Plain.* I'll write the title on the whiteboard for those of you who need to see it. Once you have found the title and the page where it begins, please turn to that page." He circulates and provides help as needed. Once all the students have found the story, Josh invites them to do a two-minute picture walk while he does a brief think-aloud along the way, showing how a reader can warm up to reading a text. Looking at the picture of Ki-Pat standing on one leg, he comments, "I wonder why that boy is standing on one leg? Maybe the author will tell me." After providing

Notice Josh's use of an independent picture walk and a pause in his instruction, giving students time to think. These techniques provide learners an opportunity to gather and process "facts" to apply to their understanding, which is attending to the need to engage learners in multiple ways.

students with a couple of minutes for the picture walk, students are given time to share with their neighbors some predictions about the folktale. He calls on partners to state their responses, and he writes them on the whiteboard. After he writes the prediction on the board, he invites all students to chorally read back the predictions. Finally, before students begin to read the text, Josh gives each student a four-box grid. He displays sentences from the story to help students with both the pronunciation and understanding of words that might pose difficulties. He comments, "As I was thinking about having you read this folktale, I found a few words that might trip you up so let's take a look at them now before you start reading. I have each of them in these sentences." He displays the sentences on a chart large enough for all to see and tells students to attempt reading them on their own. He then reads the sentences to students and asks them to copy each of the underlined words in a box on their grid. He then asks each student to draw a little picture that will help them remember the word. He quickly roams around the room to check their understanding of the words.

> *Within this section of his lesson plan, Josh continually applies multiple methods of presentation and engagement. This is evident through chorally reading student predictions and sentences that are also displayed (on the chart, whiteboard, etc.).*

> *Both students' needs and strengths are attended to as Josh uses both the writing within the grid as well as the creation of pictures to remember word meanings. These methods exemplify excellent options for effective presentation, expression, and engagement.*

"OK," Josh says. "I think you're set for reading this folktale. Once you are finished, remember to respond to your reading by filling in your own folktale grid so you can see which elements are included in this folktale."

Reading and Responding

Josh tells students that most of them will be reading the story to themselves and that others will be reading it with him. But before he has students begin reading, he sets clear expectations for all by saying, "We all read at different speeds and this is natural when we are reading silently. To show respect for all learners in the room and to get as much time for reading as possible, here's what you need to do if you finish reading and responding before others or before I finish reading and responding with some students." He refers students to the posted directions. (See Figure 3–5.)

Figure 3–5 *Directions for Continued Reading*

Directions for Continued Reading

If you are finished reading and responding before others . . .

1. Read another folktale displayed on the folktale shelves in the classroom library.

2. Reread this folktale.

3. Reread the other folktales you have read in this anthology.

> *Take note of the continued use of reading aloud and calling attention to the rhyme and rhythm used repeatedly within the text. Multiple learners, especially ELLs, will be much more successful in their independent silent reading due to this support.*

Josh now provides time for students to independently read the story silently and respond to it by completing their own folktale grid. Once students are engaged, he calls together those students who will need additional support. He begins by reviewing the sentences that contain words that might pose difficulty. They go back over the students' word grids. He then models how to read the text by reading the first page aloud. He points out how rhyme and rhythm are used and how both should help them as they read. He also walks them through the rest of the story, showing them how it repeats and how the stanzas build on one another. He then asks students to attempt to read the text on their own, reading it silently while he observes and helps individual students as needed. Once all students are finished reading, they complete their folktale grids in their literature response logs. Josh sees that they have little difficulty completing this response activity so he disbands the group and has them finish it at their desks while he monitors others in the room.

Extending

Josh calls the students together. He has a lot of ideas for extending this lesson and he begins by reviewing. While pointing to the class folktale grid, he says, "So today we read *Bringing the Rain to Kapiti Plain*. I am going to write the title right here." He writes the title in the appropriate place on the grid. He then proceeds by asking which elements are in the folktale and places a check mark in the cell to indicate that that particular element was

Notice how Josh reviews the elements of the folktale by checking these off within the grid. This provides an option for engagement with the lesson that fits many learners' needs. In addition, he addresses multiple methods of demonstrating knowledge as students produce the list of what is now known about plains.

evident. He then reviews the landforms that were evident in the folktale and has students generate a list of what they know about plains. Finally, he reminds students of the additional folktales that they can read during their self-selected independent reading time. That's about all he has time for today but he will continue the extension tomorrow.

Here's what he has planned: He will home in on having students practice reading to better understand prosodic features of language (i.e., phrasing, intonation, expression). Refer back to Day 2 in the extension part of Josh's lesson shown in Figure 3–3 (pages 38–39) for Josh's specific directions to the students.

Josh's conclusion of the lesson with reference to additional folktales provides opportunities for self-directed discovery of patterns found among folktales. This is a flexible option that helps students be challenged and stay motivated.

Illustration of an Intermediate Grade Lesson

Ginny believes that Patricia Reilly Giff's book *Nory Ryan's Song* is a good common text to use at the beginning of a unit focused on immigration. (See Figure 3–6.) Ginny wants all of her students to explore their roots and heritage and launches the exploration with this story of the Irish immigrants. By getting this book "into the heads" of all of her students, she believes it can be used as an anchor book for future instruction, provide an opportunity to model and practice classroom routines, and build community across the class by experiencing the same text. Its narrative story line allows for reviewing and improving her students' understanding of narrative story elements (setting, character, conflict), which should help aid comprehension and composition performances.

Frontloading

Ginny asks all students to create a chart in their learning logs by drawing three columns as she produces a similar structure on a large sheet of poster paper at the front of the class. She asks students to listen as she reads aloud from the first part of chapter 1 of *Nory Ryan's Song* to the whole class. She

Figure 3–6 *Ginny's Grouping Without Tracking Lesson Plan*

Content Area: Social Studies **Content Objective:** To understand the immigration experience. **Comprehension Objective:** To use story grammar to better understand elements of character, setting, and conflict.	
Text(s)	*Nory Ryan's Song* (Patricia Reilly Giff 2000). New York: Scholastic. ISBN: 0439444357.

Frontloading (Before Reading)
 	
• **Whole Class**
	1. Instruct students to create a chart in their learning logs that replicates the three-column chart the teacher produced on poster paper large enough for all to see.
	2. Read aloud the first part of chapter 1 to the entire class.
	3. After reading, label three columns on the chart paper with these headings: setting, characters, tensions.
	4. Think aloud to emphasize the importance of identifying details related to setting, characters, and tensions to better comprehend the story.
	5. Write what was gleaned about the setting, characters, and tensions from the first part of the story on the chart.
	6. Remind students to listen for and read for how authors provide clues about the setting, characters, and tensions so that they can not only better understand the story but also use the same kind of clues when they write stories.
	7. Write the clues detected and details on the large chart.
	8. Provide students time to write the information shown on the large class chart on their individual charts in their learning logs.
	9. Repeat steps two through eight using the next sections of chapter 1 following a gradual release format:
	  • Teacher and students read and respond together.
	  • Students read more independently with teacher prompting responses.
	  • Students read and respond independently while teacher monitors.
	10. To review the chapter, divide students into three groups. Group 1 will read Nory's lines, group 2 Sean's lines, and group 3 narration. Provide students time to silently read their lines and then do an impromptu readers' theatre by having the groups read aloud their lines when appropriate.
	11. Once they are finished reading, ask students to check their chart for any details they forgot to add about the setting, characters, and tensions in the story.

Figure 3–6 *Continued*

45

*Model 1: Grouping
Without Tracking*

Reading and Responding (During Reading)
 	
• Groups
	1. Provide students with directions for reading chapter 2:
	   • Silently read chapter 2.
	   • Show your response to the chapter by adding it to your three-column chart.
	  If you finish reading before the others:
	   • Talk with a partner about what you read and discovered.
	   • Read additional resources about immigration shown on the display shelf in classroom library.
	   • Read additional books by Reilly Giff shown on the display shelf in classroom library.
	2. As students independently read, gather the students who need additional help with this grade-level text to the reading table to provide them with additional reading and writing support.

Extending (After Reading)	1. Reconvene the whole class. 2. Form triads so that students can share what they have read and discovered. Make sure that triads reflect mixed achievement levels with narrow ranges. 3. Prepare triads to report out by reminding them that reporters will be picked randomly. Strategically call on students from each triad to share information that can be added to the class chart. Include as many voices as possible. 4. Collect students' learning logs. Look to see how well those students who were independently reading and responding were able to identify ideas related to setting, characters, and tensions. 5. Provide time for students who were reading and responding in the support group to independently read additional resources on immigration. Remind them to choose something that is at their just-right reading level. (This is text that they should be able to understand without the help of others.) 6. Talk with those students who read chapter 2 independently about other books they are beginning to read.

stops after reading and asks students to label the three columns: setting, characters, and tensions. (See Figure 3–7.) She labels the three columns on the poster paper and uses a think-aloud to reveal the importance in noting details about the setting, characters, and tensions to help with understanding the story. Ginny reminds the students to observe how writers reveal clues about their settings, characters, and tensions and to try to use those

Figure 3–7 Nory Ryan's Song *Chart*

Nory Ryan's Song			
Setting	Characters	Tensions	

Notice Ginny's technique of displaying the three-column notes and using them to structure her think-aloud and read-aloud. This is an effective method of presentation and option for engagement in the lesson that will meet multiple learners' needs.

models when they are writing their stories. She then reveals what she learned about the setting, characters, and tensions of this story from the first part that she read. Some information was explicitly told by the author. Other information required Ginny to use inferences from what was written. Ginny writes clues and details on the large poster paper and invites students to fill in their charts with her. She repeats the process but asks the students to listen to the next section of the first chapter and then add more clues to their charts as they learn more about the setting, characters, and tensions. She then invites the students to read the next part with her noting additional details after the choral reading. Finally, she asks the students to read the next section on their own adding to their graphic organizer. They work together in the large group to share and record what they are discovering. After working through the first chapter, she asks all students to open up their texts. She quickly divides the class into three groups. One group is assigned to read Nory's lines, the second reads her friend Sean's lines, and the third reads the narration along with her. The class does an impromptu readers' theatre to review the first chapter. After the readers' theatre, they return to their charts and check if there are any other details they forgot to add about the setting, characters, and tensions in the story.

Reading and Responding

Ginny has now reached the point in the lesson where she is ready to turn the reading and response to the next chapter in the book over to her students. She defines the independent work as reading chapter 2 and responding to the text by continuing to add to their charts as they read or after they read. Ginny reminds the students of their rules for doing independent work and what they can do when they are all done with their work—share what they have read and written with a buddy who is also done, read from additional books by Patrica Reilly Giff, or read other resources on immigration. She monitors as the students get engaged with their independent reading and then calls a small group of students in need of more support to the table. With the small group, she reviews the narrative story elements and what has been discovered so far. She reads aloud from the second chapter and models how to spot clues and adds them to the chart. She asks the students to work along with her on their charts. Then she selects another section of the text that they can chorally read and afterward stops and discusses what they have learned. Ginny isolates one small section of the text for the students to read silently and asks them to add at least two details to their charts, monitoring their ability to complete the task independently. As time is running out, she finishes by reading the last part of the chapter aloud to the students and collectively they add a few more details to their charts.

Ginny uses multiple models of reading to, with, and by children, providing varied levels of language support for ELLs and other learners. In addition, the continued adding to the graphic organizer and acquiring facts to understand and analyze the text serves the purpose of engaging learners within the lesson. This is also valuable beyond the lesson because students will use this graphic organizer in their acquisition of more information that connects to these concepts.

Notice how this flexible option for engagement meets learners' needs with this grouping without tracking model. Time to read independently and opportunities for self-directed discovery allows these learners to feel comfortable, interested, and yet challenged as well.

Extending

The teacher brings the class back together. She has strategically arranged the students in mixed achievement triads being careful to keep the gaps as narrow as possible. Students share with their partners what they have read and what they are learning about the setting, characters, and tensions in this novel. She informs the triads that each group will have to be ready to add to the charts. Ginny reminds the students that she will randomly pick their reporter, so each triad needs to make sure every member is prepared to share. The class comes back together as a large group to add to the poster paper chart. She systematically calls on students to include as many voices as possible. After the discussion, she collects the response journals of the students who had worked independently to check for understanding and engagement. She invites those students who had worked at the table directly with the teacher to spend a few minutes reading their extra dog storybooks selected to be more at their levels. She then engages the other students in conversations about the other Reilly Giff books and immigration resources they are reading.

> *Take note of the efforts Ginny has focused on the formation of triads. In order for all students to benefit from this small-group work, Ginny understands that various students come with needs and assets that will be attended to as she minimizes gaps and creates success through collaboration.*

Additional Resources

Cumulative Titles

Title	Author	Publisher/Year ISBN
The Apple Pie That Papa Baked	Lauren Thompson	Simon & Schuster/2007 139781416912408
The Bag I'm Taking to Grandma's	Shirley Neitzel	Greenwillow/1995 0688129609
Here Is the Arctic Winter	Madeleine Dunphy	Hyperion/1993 156282337X

Title	Author	Publisher/Year ISBN
Here Is the Southwestern Desert	Madeleine Dunphy	Hyperion/1995 0786800496
Here Is the Tropical Rainforest	Madeleine Dunphy	Hyperion/1994 1562826360

Patricia Reilly Giff Titles

Title	Publisher/Year ISBN
A House of Tailors	Wendy Lamb Books/Random House/2006 0385730667
Lily's Crossing	Yearling/1999 0440414539
Maggie's Door	Wendy Lamb Books/Random House/2005 0385326580
Pictures of Hollis Woods	Wendy Lamb Books/Random House/2002 0385326556
Water Street	Wendy Lamb Books/Random House/2006 0385730683
Willow Run	Wendy Lamb Books/Random House/2007 0440238013

Texts on Immigration

Title	Author	Publisher/Year ISBN
A Coal Miner's Bride: The Diary of Anetka Kaminska	Susan Campbell Bartoletti	Amazon Remainders Account/2000 0439053862
A House of Tailors	Patricia Reilly Giff	Wendy Lamb Books/ Random House/2006 0385730667

Title	Author	Publisher/Year ISBN
Immigrant Kids	Russell Freedman	Puffin/1995 0140375945
Island of Hope: The Journey to America and the Ellis Island Experience	Martin Sandler	Scholastic Nonfiction/2004 0439530822
Maggie's Door	Patricia Reilly Giff	Wendy Lamb Books/ Random House/2005 0385326580
Water Street	Patricia Reilly Giff	Wendy Lamb Books/ Random House/2006 0385730683
When Jessie Came Across the Sea	Amy Hest	Candlewick/2003 076361274X

Model 2: Jigsawing

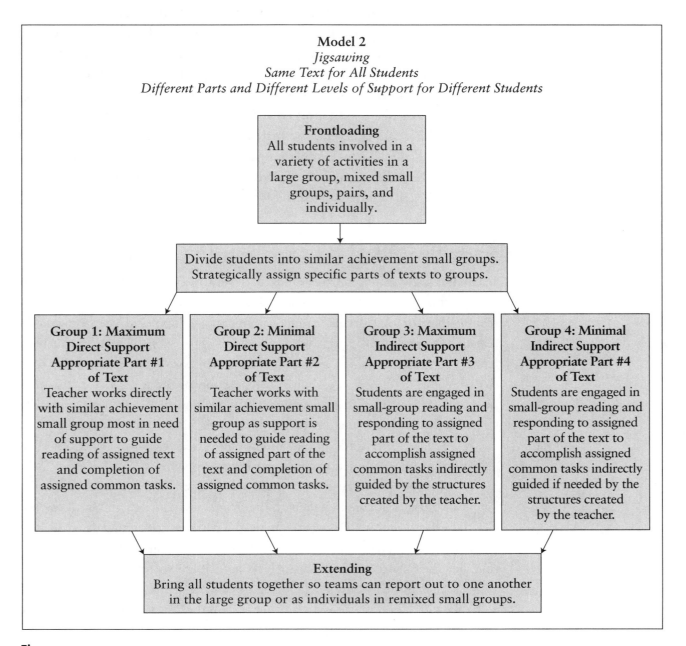

Model 2
Jigsawing
Same Text for All Students
Different Parts and Different Levels of Support for Different Students

Frontloading
All students involved in a variety of activities in a large group, mixed small groups, pairs, and individually.

Divide students into similar achievement small groups. Strategically assign specific parts of texts to groups.

Group 1: Maximum Direct Support Appropriate Part #1 of Text
Teacher works directly with similar achievement small group most in need of support to guide reading of assigned text and completion of assigned common tasks.

Group 2: Minimal Direct Support Appropriate Part #2 of Text
Teacher works with similar achievement small group as support is needed to guide reading of assigned part of the text and completion of assigned common tasks.

Group 3: Maximum Indirect Support Appropriate Part #3 of Text
Students are engaged in small-group reading and responding to assigned part of the text to accomplish assigned common tasks indirectly guided by the structures created by the teacher.

Group 4: Minimal Indirect Support Appropriate Part #4 of Text
Students are engaged in small-group reading and responding to assigned part of the text to accomplish assigned common tasks indirectly guided if needed by the structures created by the teacher.

Extending
Bring all students together so teams can report out to one another in the large group or as individuals in remixed small groups.

Figure 4–1

Scenario

In planning for this week's science lessons, you take a look at the informational text you want your students to read. Thinking about the text length and apparent difficulty level and what you know about your students helps you to realize that you are going to have to think through your instruction carefully so that all students meet with reading success. Upon closer inspection of the text, you notice that it is has been formatted into different sections, clearly marked by the boldfaced headings for each section. This format leads you to see that you can easily divide the reading into smaller pieces. When you look at these different sections, you see that some appear more difficult than others both in terms of length and the way that the information is represented. In some sections, for example, the author uses visuals to help the reader better understand the accompanying narrative. These sections will most likely be more manageable for students who struggle with reading long passages and need some support with diagrams. Other parts will help you to challenge those students who can read with relative ease yet need to learn to build reading stamina by reading longer passages. Text sections and student success at the forefront of your mind, you decide to use jigsawing, a technique you heard about at a recent differentiation workshop.

Explanation

Jigsawing grew in popularity as one of several ways to implement cooperative learning. The basic premise behind jigsawing is that each group is responsible for one predetermined chunk of the text and each reports its learnings to the other groups who read other chunks of the text. In this way, learners contribute to one another's knowledge base while at the same time experiencing reading success with their portion of the text. While it cannot be used with every text, jigsawing lends itself well to any text primarily structured as a main idea with supporting details, which is often true of many informational trade books and content-area textbook selections such as the science text alluded to in the opening scenario.

As illustrated in Figure 4–1, when using jigsawing, the teacher usually keeps all of the students together on the front, or at the beginning, of the lesson (i.e., frontloading). Doing so enables all learners to see that regardless of perceived reading level, each is part of the same learning community and that together they share a common goal: to contribute to one another's knowledge as a result of reading and sharing information that others have not had a chance to read on their own. Another reason that the lesson begins with the whole class is that whole-group instruction saves time. It affords the teacher the opportunity to build the background, vocabulary, and strategies that students need to be able to handle the text individually and as a team.

Once the frontloading part of the lesson with the whole class is completed, the teacher proceeds to the next part of the lesson, which calls on students to read and respond to the text. The teacher has divided the text into a manageable number of meaningful chunks and has made some decisions about which group will get which chunk of text. In other words, the teacher strategically forms groups by matching each chunk of the text with an appropriate group. Chunks might vary in length, conceptual load, vocabulary, potential interest, and other factors such as graphic organizers that might make one chunk easier to read than another. This careful group formation and text matching is a way of setting all learners up for reading success. Beside differentiating by using different parts of the text for different groups, the teacher can also enhance differentiation by providing more support for any group that may be struggling to learn from its part of the selection.

Finally, once each group has read and responded to its chunk of the text, the teacher proceeds to the last part of the lesson. This is when you reorganize the class so that groups or individuals can share what they have learned with others. Figure 4–2 shows the key elements of jigsawing and a brief explanation of each element.

General Teaching Suggestions

Preparation

1. Select a text that can be divided easily and that allows for multiple levels of reading.

2. Plan prereading activities that will adequately frontload the lesson for all readers. Focus on standards-based skills and strategies and/ or content needed by your students as revealed in your ongoing assessments.

3. Carefully consider how to match sections of text to homogenous groups of students.

4. Plan group-response activities that will engage students as they work together. Build on instruction during the frontloading of the lesson.

5. Be prepared to provide support to any group that may require additional teacher guidance.

Figure 4-2 *Key Elements of Jigsawing*

Key Elements	Jigsawing Model
Text	Use different parts of the same text for different groups of students. Textbooks lend themselves well to jigsawing as do children's books such as Nancy Luenn's *Celebration of Light* (Atheneum, 1998).
Grouping	Use connected small groups, partners, and/or individual reading for the actual reading and responding to text but also include the use of the whole class to frontload and conclude the lesson.
Differentiation	Predetermined parts of the texts are assigned to better match the performance levels of the students; additional differentiation may include varying the level of support from the teacher for each group. Differentiation also occurs as a result of the teaching/learning activities. For example, brainstorming appeals to students who are auditory learners and those who are more linguistic whereas a colorful visual display appeals to visual learners and to those who remember information because of the artistic display. Written responses appeal to those learners who are tactile and kinesthetic as well as those who learn best by taking the time to formulate their ideas and put them in written form.
Best Uses	When the common text being used by all learners in the classroom community is easily divisible into chunks at various levels such as nonfiction and informational tradebooks, textbook selections, and/or class magazines and newspapers.
Advantages	• It builds community across the classroom by providing shared experiences. • It requires a limited amount of materials. • It allows you to provide support to those who need it while others are kept engaged with similar tasks.
Disadvantages	• Understanding how to divide texts into sections with various reading levels to provide appropriate reading opportunities for teams of students is an acquired skill. • Initial lesson preparation can be more time consuming. • Students must be well prepared to work effectively as teams requiring an upfront investment of time and energy.

6. Plan extension activities that bring the class together as a community of learners. Continue to build on previous instruction. Consider how extension activities may lead to additional inquiry opportunities.

7. Plan for an evaluation of work habits of individuals within groups to strengthen skills for use beyond the lesson.

8. Remember to plan a variety of activities so that you can provide for learner differences as an integral part of the lesson. For example, using a graphic organizer is sure to capture the attention of visual learners whereas using colors will help those learners who are more

artistically inclined to focus and remember the information. Having students work and talk with others in small groups garners the attention of learners who learn best by listening to others and feeling part of a team.

Frontloading

1. Activate schema about the text. Make sure all students are thinking about the topic.

2. Develop needed background knowledge for the text.

3. Address any skills and strategies including vocabulary needed to successfully read the text.

4. Generate interest about the text.

5. "Walk" through the text with the students pointing out the various sections of the text. Outline or graphically represent the organization of the text.

6. Select the first part of the section of the text to read aloud to the students. As you are reading the first part, model how to do the response activity. As appropriate, have the students replicate your work.

7. For guided practice, invite all students to read the middle part of that section of the text using choral reading or an informal readers' theatre. As they are reading the second part with you, invite the students to tell you how to add to the response activity. As appropriate, have students add to their work.

8. For independent practice, invite all students to read the final part of that section of the text on their own while still in the large group. Focus their reading and follow up to see that the purpose was accomplished. As they are reading the third part on their own, monitor if they can add to the response activity without you.

9. Identify group members for each of the remaining sections of the text.

10. Provide visible written directions for work to be done by the groups.

Reading and Responding

1. Turn the completion of the task modeled and practiced during the frontloading over to the groups:

   * Review the directions as needed.

   * Review any class rules as needed about working together as groups.

   * Clearly identify one or two activities that the students can do when they are finished reading and responding (e.g., skim other parts of the text, study additional displayed texts).

   * Monitor the groups to ensure that they get successfully started on the reading and response activity.

2. Once the groups seem engaged in their independent work, work with the group that needs additional support in the identified place in your classroom.

   * Review any of the frontloading activities as needed.

   * Address any other critical skills more appropriate for this group.

   * Assist them in the reading of the text. Since they should have been assigned a more appropriate part of the text, encourage them to read on their own as much as possible.

   * Provide support in completing the response activity including additional modeling and guided practice as needed.

   * Be intentional about identifying at least part of the response activity that the group can complete on its own.

   * Prepare the students to share what they have learned with the whole class.

Extending

1. Instruct each group to report what it has learned from its assigned section of the text to the other groups.

2. Spend time asking the students to complete self-evaluations. Students can discuss something that went well in their group and something that they could improve on next time. Use their comments to improve on succeeding jigsawing lessons.

Illustration of a Primary Lesson

Christine's third graders have been learning about different cultures as part of their social studies curriculum. To further students' understanding about how cultures are alike and different, she decides to augment the social studies textbook by using an informational children's literature selection, *Celebration of Light* (Luenn 1998). She believes that the jigsawing grouping structure will lend itself well to this lesson. The book's format will make it easy for her to pair up students to read about different countries. Likewise, the text for each country is relatively brief so students should have little difficulty with it. They will be able to focus more on reading to look for specific information that highlights how cultural groups are alike and different. See Figure 4–3 for her completed lesson plan (and Appendix B for a blank Jigsaw Lesson Plan form.)

Frontloading

Christine opens the lesson by gathering all students in the meeting area so that all can see the whiteboard and the world map. She reminds students that they have been learning about similarities and differences among different cultural groups and that they are going to use an informational book to add to what they have been learning in their social studies text. She writes the word *light* on the whiteboard and asks, "When you think of the word *light*, what words come to mind? Please use your sticky note pad to write your words. Use one sticky note for each word."

> *Notice Christine's use of sticky notes to elicit active student engagement in the lesson as well as the requirement of one-word responses, which supports students with a variety of language needs.*

> *The arrangement of words into categories on the board provides an effective method of presenting information and using the knowledge that students have demonstrated, causing increased interest in and motivation to remain focused within the lesson.*

Responses recorded, Christine asks students to pair up with the person sitting next to them and to share their words. She then tells students to choose a word they would like to display on the board saying, "Now that you have shared your words, choose one that you might like to put on the whiteboard." In an orderly manner, volunteers come to the board and display their self-selected word. After a few words are displayed, Christine arranges them into logical categories (e.g., objects associated with

Figure 4-3 *Christine's Jigsaw Lesson Plan*

Content Area: Social Studies **Content Objective:** To identify likenesses and differences among different cultural groups. **Comprehension Objective:** To identify and describe how different cultures honor and celebrate light.	
Text(s)	*Celebration of Light* (Nancy Luenn 1998). New York: Atheneum. ISBN: 068931986.
Frontloading (Before Reading) • **Whole Class**	1. Gather all students in the meeting area so that they can see the whiteboard and the world map. 2. Write the word *light* on the board and have students brainstorm words they associate with light, putting each in logical categories (e.g., objects associated with light, uses of light). 3. Point to the world map saying something like, "Light has become something that is celebrated throughout the world. Today, you're going to read about how people from different parts of the world celebrate light." 4. Read the introduction aloud. 5. Explain to students that they will be reading about different countries and identifying how the people from each country celebrate light. Students will show their understanding of their country by filling in the three-column chart. (See Figure 4–4.) 6. Demonstrate how to fill out the three-column chart by reading about Brazil and completing the chart displayed large enough for all to see. "So that others know which country I am talking about, I am going to write *Brazil* in the space at the top of the chart. The first column asks me to write the time of year. Let's see. It says right here." Continue this way until the entire chart is completed. 7. Tell students that they will be working with partners to learn about their assigned country.
Reading and Responding (During Reading) • **Partners**	1. Randomly pair students and give each pair the reading passage for different countries. Also give them the three-column chart to complete. 2. Provide written directions as a reminder for what partners are to do. (See Figure 4–5.) 3. Provide time for partners to read about their country and write on their charts. 4. As partners read and write, circulate and help as needed. Some partners may need additional help with understanding how to identify the information and where to write it on the chart.

Figure 4–3 *Continued* **59**

Extending (After Reading) • **Whole Class**	1. Bring all partners together.
	2. In turn, have students locate their assigned country on the world map and have them place a pushpin on the name of the country. Then ask partners to share the information with the class about light as noted on their charts.
	3. To better understand likenesses and differences among the countries, complete the semantic features analysis grid. (See Figure 4–6.)

light, uses of light). She then shifts students' attention to the world map commenting, "You have a lot of ideas about light and so do people around the world. Today you're going to discover how different people think about light. Just by taking a look at how they think about light, you'll see how people are alike and different."

Christine then shows students the three-column chart that they will be using to record information they discover about their country (see Figure 4–4) and uses Brazil, the first country, to model the entire process saying, "This is the chart you are going to use to record information you discover. Let me show you how to complete it. First, write the name of the country that is shown at the top of your text. Mine says *Brazil* so I am going to write Brazil in the space next to the word *Country*. I need to read this text before I can fill out the rest of the chart." She displays a copy of the text on the overhead transparency so that all can see it and pauses to read it to herself. Pointing to the text, she comments, "Let's see, it says here that light is celebrated in January so I will write that in the first column." She continues showing students where she obtained the information about when and why light is celebrated by underlining it with an overhead pen and then writing it in the appropriate column.

The auditory explanations of expectations paired with the visual representation of the appropriate ways to complete the activity contribute to the variety of ways students can acquire information within this lesson.

She continues, "Now that you have seen me do this on my own, let's try it together with another country." She displays a second transparency that shows the text for China and gives students a copy that they can read and make their own by writing on it. "Go ahead and read the text, just like I did, and see if you can find the information that you need to fill in the chart. You can work with a partner if you would like." After students have had some time to try out the reading and writing, she calls them back together saying,

Figure 4-4 *Attribute Table*

Country _____		
Time of year light is celebrated	How light is celebrated	Why light is celebrated

"Ok, now help me fill in the chart." As volunteers provide responses, she fills in the chart. She also has volunteers use the overhead pen to underline the information they discovered in the text for each section on the chart. She closes this part of the lesson saying, "Now that you have had some practice with how you need to read and identify information, I think you are ready to read on your own."

Reading and Responding

Christine tells students that they will be working with partners when reading about a country and completing the informational chart. She provides them with written instructions as a reminder of the expectations. (See Figure 4–5.) Because Christine knows that the text for some of the countries is more complex than others, she has matched specific countries with students so

Although seemingly simple, Christine's decision to have students working in pairs as opposed to independently is an important one. This grouping provides ELLs with support from peers as well as opportunities to engage in both oral and written language in a more comfortable environment in which students are more likely to take risks.

Directions for Reading and Responding

1. Each partner reads silently. If you need help with something, you can ask your partner.

2. Once you have read, take turns to complete the chart. One person can state information while the other writes. Then change jobs so that you get to be a reporter and a writer.

---

that all students will meet with reading success. She presents a chart that lists the name of the country on the left and the two students who will be reading about that country to the right of the country. She also gives each pair one response chart to complete. Once students are situated, they begin reading and Christine circulates stopping to help individuals and partners as needed.

Extending

Once Christine sees that all partners have completed the reading and their charts, she calls them back together as a whole class. In turn, she asks partners to state the name of their country and to locate it on the world map with a pushpin. She then asks students to share what they discovered about their country.

Notice how the use of pushpins on the world map serves multiple purposes here. Students are not only given the opportunity to demonstrate their knowledge in kinesthetic and visual ways but all students in the class benefit from this visual representation and therefore remain both interested and motivated as they listen to their peers.

Once all partners have shared, Christine uses a semantic features analysis grid (see Figure 4–6) to help children better understand how the different countries are alike and different with respect to how they treat light. She writes the names of the countries across the top of the grid and the months of the year down the lefthand side. Christine states, "Sometimes you can use a grid like this to compare and contrast different ideas. Let me show you how this works for today's reading." She then states the name of the country and asks students when that country celebrates light, placing a check mark in the corresponding cell. She continues in like manner until the grid is complete and comments, "Just by looking at this

Figure 4-6 *Semantic Features Grid*

	Brazil	China	Sweden	United States
January	✓	✓		✓
February		✓		
March				
April				
May				
June				
July				
August				
September				
October				
November				
December	✓		✓	✓

The use of the semantic feature analysis grid demonstrates Christine's understanding of the need to not only synthesize information that had been presented, but also to do so in a way that is not dependent on language only. ELLs in particular will be better able to understand and retain information presented in this way.

grid, I can see which countries celebrate light during the same time of the year and those that don't. Take a look at January, for example. All of the countries that celebrate light during that month have a check mark in the column." To make sure students understand how to read the grid, she calls out months at random and asks students to note which countries celebrate light during that month. She concludes the lesson stating, "Our goal today was to discover likeness and differences among people across the world. We did this by having you take a look at how people from different countries celebrate light. You now have some additional information about how countries are alike and different."

Illustration of an Intermediate Grade Lesson

Janelle's fifth-grade students have been studying ecosystems and how to identify significant details simultaneously. While she has seen some progress, she realizes that students still need some practice with identifying elements of the ocean's ecosystem, in this case whales. To help her accomplish this objective, she decides to use the jigsawing structure. See Figure 4–7 for her lesson plan.

Frontloading

Janelle opens the lesson by telling students that they are going to add to what they have already learned about the ocean ecosphere. She begins to draw an information web on the whiteboard. She asks the students to replicate her work in their learning logs. In the center circle, she writes the question "What is a whale?" She asks students to write two or three answers they know or think they know for the question in the center circle in their learning logs. Students then partner up to pair-share their ideas. After this partner work, Janelle asks for volunteers to state ideas that she then adds to the web on the whiteboard. Janelle then reads aloud the introduction to Chapter 2 from the text. Using a think-aloud to model what students are supposed to do when they read, she adds new information to the central circle saying, "I see! The author says that whales are as big as a city bus. I think this is an important detail to add to the web."

Now Janelle asks the students to look at Chapter 2 and scan for the next heading in the book. She models how to add a circle to the information web and how to write the heading *Is a Whale a Fish?* inside it. Students continue scanning until they discover the next heading *Whales on Land* and add it to another circle on the information web. The scanning continues as they add three more circles and headings to the information webs.

> *Janelle has addressed a variety of differentiation techniques with her use and structuring of the learning logs. First, the use of an information web, showing connections to a central idea, as well as the pair-share of the ideas recorded here afford opportunities for students to demonstrate their knowledge in multiple ways (i.e., visually and orally) while remaining challenged and actively engaged in this frontloading section of her lesson.*

Reading and Responding

Janelle is now ready to provide directions for completing today's reading. She informs the students that they will work in groups to read separate sections

Figure 4–7 *Janelle's Jigsaw Lesson Plan*

Content Area: Science **Content Objective:** To identify attributes of whales. **Comprehension Objective:** To summarize information about whales.	
Text(s)	*Whales and Dolphins,* chapter 2 of Explorer Books (Della Rowland 1991). New York: Trumpet Club. ISBN: 0440843510.
Frontloading (Before Reading) • **Whole Class**	1. Tell students that they are going to add some information to what they already know about the ocean ecosphere. 2. Draw an information web on the whiteboard and ask that students do the same in their individual learning logs. 3. Write "What is a whale?" in the center of the web, and ask students to write down two or three answers. 4. Pair up students and have them share ideas. 5. Ask for volunteers to add responses and add them to the class web shown on the whiteboard. 6. Read aloud the introduction to chapter 2 using a think-aloud to add information to the web: "I see! The author says that whales are as big as a city bus. I think this is an important detail to add to the web." 7. Provide time for students to look through chapter 2 and identify the next heading. Add it to the web as a spoke off of the center. Continue in like manner until all sections have been identified and are shown on the web. 8. Tell students that they will work in teams to read the different sections of the chapter that correspond to the headings on the web. 9. Tell students that they will need to identify what they think is important information for others to know about their section and that they will write their ideas on the class web as they share their ideas. 10. Show students the grouping chart that shows which group they are in to complete the activity. 11. Provide written directions so that each group knows what to do. (Refer to Figure 4–9.)
Reading and Responding (During Reading) • **Groups**	1. Provide time for teams to silently read their text sections. 2. As groups read, circulate and help as needed. Some teams may need specific help with identifying ideas that will be added to the class web. 3. Monitor to make sure that all groups feel comfortable with what they have identified to share with the rest of the class. Provide help as needed.

Figure 4–7 *Continued*

65

Model 2: Jigsawing

Extending (After Reading) • Whole Class	1. Bring all groups together. 2. In turn, have the reporter from each group add information to the appropriate section on the web. 3. When listening to the presentation, all others are also writing the shared information in their own response logs. 4. After each group reporter is finished sharing information, provide time for others to ask any related questions. 5. Once all group reporters have shared, instruct each student to complete a THNK-WINK. 6. Have students share their THNK-WINKs with a partner. 7. Ask for a few volunteers to share their WINKs and list them on the board for all to see. 8. Conclude the lesson by having students reflect on the small-group experience: What went well? What might need to be improved?

of the chapter adding significant details about whales they have learned from their sections to the information web. Once all groups have finished studying their sections, the class will work together to teach each other critical information about the whales. She displays the grouping chart that shows the group members and their assigned sections (see Figure 4–8, Grouping Chart) and another chart with written directions for completing the reading and responding activities (see Figure 4–9, Transparency).

Directions displayed, Janelle provides time for groups to silently read their text sections.

As the groups read, she circulates and helps as needed. Some groups need specific help with identifying ideas that will be added to the class web. She stops and works with these groups. As the reading and responding progresses and the group she is helping seems to better understand what they are to accomplish, she leaves the group and monitors other groups to make sure that all groups feel comfortable with what they have identified to share with the rest of the class.

Note the design of the group activity described in Figure 4–9. Within this activity, Janelle has provided flexible options for engagement in her decision to have students read and respond independently, followed up by negotiation as a group to determine the most important points to share with the whole class. This challenges students to focus on their own reading strategies, while staying motivated to contribute to the group.

Figure 4–8 *Grouping Chart*

Section Title: _____ Group Members:	Section Title: _____ Group Members:
Section Title: _____ Group Members:	Section Title: _____ Group Members:

Figure 4–9 *Transparency*

Directions for Reading and Responding

1. Silently read your sections.

2. Either during or after your reading, identify and write in your response log three ideas that you think are important to your section.

3. Once you see that others in your group are finished, share your ideas.

4. As a group, come to an agreement about the three points you will add to the whole class web shown on the whiteboard.

5. Form a list that shows your three ideas.

6. Choose a reporter to report out your three ideas to the rest of the class.

7. If you get finished before I call you back together as a whole class:
    - Look at other displayed books.
    - Reread your section.
    - Skim other sections of the chapter.

Once Janelle sees that all groups have finished identifying their ideas, she brings all the groups together. In turn, she invites the reporter from each group to add information to the appropriate section on the web. She also provides additional directions for the listeners saying, "After the information is written on the web, you need to write it in your individual literature response logs. When we are finished today, your individual webs should look exactly like the one that is shown here on the whiteboard."

After each group reporter is finished sharing information, Janelle provides time for others to ask any related questions. She comments, "Now that you have heard about this section of the text, what, if any, additional questions do you have of this group?" No questions might emerge but she wants to provide this time just in case there are some that are lurking.

As the lesson comes to a close, Janelle asks all students to fold a piece of paper lengthwise, open it, and draw a line down the middle. In the lefthand column, she asks the students to write THNK (Things I Now Know) and WINK (What I Need to Know) on the right. She states, "Go ahead and write one or two ideas in the THNK column and one or two questions in the WINK column." She then has students partner up and share their THNK-WINKs. Volunteers then state some of their WINKs and Janelle records them on the whiteboard next to the information web. She concludes

Janelle's use of the THNK-WINK chart exemplifies an effective way for students to demonstrate the knowledge they've synthesized throughout the lesson, and provides information for further teaching based on student interest, which continues to engage her students in the content.

the lesson by stating, "Today we had a couple of goals in mind. One was to learn more about the ocean ecosystem. We did this by reading about one type of animal that lives in the ocean. You also showed that you were able to identify important information and share it with others. One last activity for you to do today is this. In your response logs, please reflect on your group experience by answering these two questions: What went well? What might need to be improved?" She writes the two questions on the board and provides students with time to write.

Additional Resources

Sample Children's Literature Titles Suitable for Jigsawing

Title	Author	Publisher/Year ISBN	Suggested Grade Levels
Amazing Dinosaurs: More Feathers, More Claws, Big Horns, Wide Jaws!	Dougal Dixon	Boyds Mills Press/ 2007 9781590785379	2–4
Animals Nobody Loves	Seymour Simon	Sea Star/2001 1587170795	3
Did It Take Creativity to Find Relativity, Albert Einstein? (one of several in the Scholastic SuperGiants Series)	Melvin and Gilda Berger	Scholastic/2007 9780439833844	2–3
Do Tarantulas Have Teeth? Questions and Answers About Poisonous Creatures (one of several in the Scholastic Question and Answer Series)	Melvin and Gilda Berger	Scholastic/1999 9780439148771	3–4
Heroes for Civil Rights	David Adler	Holiday House/2008 9780823420087	4–5
A Horse in the House and Other Strange But True Animal Stories	Gail Ablow	Candlewick Press/ 2007 9780763628383	3–5
Space	Alan Dyer	Simon & Schuster/ 2007 14416938606	4–5
Tales of Famous Americans	Connie and Peter Roop	Scholastic/2007 9780439641166	4–5

CHAPTER 5

Model 3:
Connected Literature Circles

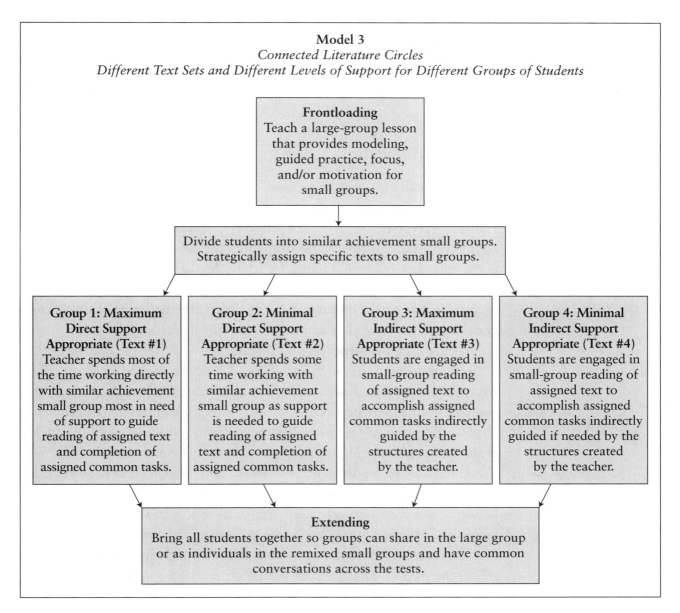

Model 3
Connected Literature Circles
Different Text Sets and Different Levels of Support for Different Groups of Students

Frontloading
Teach a large-group lesson that provides modeling, guided practice, focus, and/or motivation for small groups.

Divide students into similar achievement small groups. Strategically assign specific texts to small groups.

Group 1: Maximum Direct Support Appropriate (Text #1)
Teacher spends most of the time working directly with similar achievement small group most in need of support to guide reading of assigned text and completion of assigned common tasks.

Group 2: Minimal Direct Support Appropriate (Text #2)
Teacher spends some time working with similar achievement small group as support is needed to guide reading of assigned text and completion of assigned common tasks.

Group 3: Maximum Indirect Support Appropriate (Text #3)
Students are engaged in small-group reading of assigned text to accomplish assigned common tasks indirectly guided by the structures created by the teacher.

Group 4: Minimal Indirect Support Appropriate (Text #4)
Students are engaged in small-group reading of assigned text to accomplish assigned common tasks indirectly guided if needed by the structures created by the teacher.

Extending
Bring all students together so groups can share in the large group or as individuals in the remixed small groups and have common conversations across the tests.

Figure 5–1

Scenario

To help students understand the westward expansion included in the social studies curriculum, you decide to breathe some life into the topic. While your textbook does a good job of outlining the basics, it lacks personal stories that make history come to life and better capture students' interests. Recognizing that your students have a range of reading levels, you decide to use connected literature circles. Connected literature circles help you to engage readers because they allow you to provide similar instruction across groups and create the potential for connected conversations throughout the class. You begin by searching for multiple copies of four books about frontier life written at different levels of complexity that will match up with your students' reading levels. You form four groups of students of similar achievement and provide an appropriately matched title to each group. You will enhance your differentiation by varying the degree of support provided to each of the literature circles. While you will give some direct support, others will be guided more indirectly.

Explanation

Literature circles emerged as a classroom organizational structure as a result of teachers wanting to fully engage their students with a variety of texts (see Figure 5–1). A basic theoretical premise is that reading best takes place in a social context. Students learn from one another as they talk about the text(s) they are reading. Talking facilitates broader understanding because students bring their background experiences to the text and share it with each other during the discussion. Their different experiences shed alternate perspectives enabling all students to more fully understand the text.

In our work with teachers and literature circles over the past few years, we have discovered that literature circles have been defined by many different features, and that results in classroom implementations that run along a continuum of experiences. On one end, there are literature circles in which almost all elements are controlled by students. Students self-select texts, group membership, roles in groups, ways of responding, evaluation decisions, and how to report to others. On the other end, teachers control every aspect of the literature circles, assigning texts, groups, roles, and projects. In between, issues of who controls what leads to lots of variation in the way literature circles are organized. There are two models we have observed that may be especially conducive to differentiated instruction. In these models, the teacher retains more control so that differentiated instruction intentionally targets specific strategies, skills, and behaviors. The first model assigns text sets containing a number of multiple copies of the same text to students who have been grouped by similar achievement. The second model uses mixed achievement groups and provides different but related texts for different students within a group. In both cases, the teacher selects a text that matches the students' reading levels.

In the connected literature circles model we describe and explain in this chapter, we emphasize keeping the whole class together on the front end of the lesson so that all of the groups receive the same instruction to focus and support their work away from the teacher when reading and responding. This permits the teacher to address curricular demands that are expected for all students and/or needs that are shared by many. It also provides the possibility for classroomwide conversations across multiple texts. After all students have benefited from the focus lesson, students move into their assigned groups to read and respond to their books. Once students are in their groups reading and responding, you can decide what role to take with each group. Some groups may need monitoring; others may need direct intervention. You may want to think about your groups in terms of which ones need to be guided directly in a face-to-face manner and which ones can be guided more indirectly in a less hands-on manner. This may help you decide how to differentiate your levels of support and how much time you will need to spend with each group. At the end of the lesson, you call the groups together again so that they can converse as a class or across groups about the day's reading and responding. While their reading includes different texts, the groups focus on similar issues and ideas. This whole-group interaction allows for sharing that promises to build and foster a stronger sense of community in a classroom of diverse learners. Figure 5–2 shows the key elements of connected literature circles and a brief explanation of each element.

General Teaching Suggestions

Preparation

1. Select texts that are written at multiple levels to match the readers in the classroom yet still have a common element. You may also need to select some additional related titles (e.g., picture books and excerpts from chapter books) to use in model lessons.

2. Plan frontloading activities that will transcend the titles but connect the conversations across them. Focus on strategies defined by

Figure 5–2 *Key Elements and Descriptions of Connected Literature Circles*

Key Elements	Connected Literature Circles Model
Text	Use different levels of complexity but related groups of texts for different groups of students.
Grouping	Primarily use similar achievement small groups for reading and responding to specific texts. Use whole-class activities keeping students together at the start and end of the lesson. These activities might also include partner and independent work when appropriate. You might also choose to use mixed achievement small groups if it is possible to provide group members with texts that match their abilities.
Differentiation	Assign predetermined related texts that you have selected to match the performance levels of the members of similar achievement or mixed achievement groups. Differentiation also comes into play when varying the level of support that you provide for the various groups and individuals within groups.
Best Uses	When multiple sets of connected texts of various levels are available for use by all learners in the classroom community to collaboratively explore a common topic, theme, genre, author, element, or strategy.
Advantages	• It builds community across the classroom by providing shared experiences while matching students with texts more appropriate to their reading levels. • It uses real texts in a setting that more closely mirrors what real readers do in the real world, the world beyond school. • It adds a critical social dimension to the reading instructional program that may have a strong appeal for some students.
Disadvantages	• You must have access to and knowledge of multiple sets of texts written at various reading levels that can still provide an opportunity for connected conversations across the classroom community while at the same time making the reading experience successful for all students. • Students must be well prepared to work effectively in small groups including how to make sure they honor all voices and not privilege some while marginalizing others.

local standards and needed by the students as revealed in ongoing assessments.

3. Carefully consider how to match texts to similar achievement small groups of students.

4. Plan response activities that will engage students as they read and respond together in small groups. Build on the focus lesson taught in the prereading phase.

5. Be prepared to provide support to any small group that may require additional teacher guidance.

6. Set up a structure to meet with each literature circle to assess whether standards are being met.

7. Plan extension activities that bring the class together as a community of learners and that build on previous instruction and lead to conversations across and beyond the texts.

8. Plan for evaluation of work habits of individuals within the literature circles to strengthen work skills for use beyond the lesson.

Frontloading

1. Set a clear purpose for reading and responding to the texts.

2. Use the first part of a related text to model how you want the literature circles to read and respond to their texts for that day.

3. Continue to read the selected text, but invite students to work with you and practice the assigned activity for the day.

4. Once the students seem confident with the activity, remind students of the literature circles organization.

5. Review rules for how to work together during the literature circles.

6. Provide visible written directions for work to be done by the small groups.

Reading and Responding

1. Turn the assignment of the activity modeled and practiced during the frontloading over to the small groups to complete within their separate texts.

2. Establish the parameters for reading further in the assigned texts. Decide whether all literature circles will read for a set amount of time, a certain number of pages or chapters, or whether the separate literature circles will decide their own parameters for reading. Also decide the manner in which the reading will take place—silently or orally, separately or collectively. Decide if all groups will read in the same manner or if each separate group should make that decision.

3. Set up the parameters for the response format assigned. Decide whether response and reading will be integrated (stop and process as the group reads) or whether the groups should read first and then

respond. Also decide whether the response is done collectively or separately.

4. Clearly identify one or two activities that the students can do when they are all done with their work if other groups are still working. Students can be encouraged to read extra copies of texts they were not assigned or additional related texts that are available in the classroom.

5. Get the literature circles started on the reading and response activity. Monitor the groups as they get engaged.

6. Once the groups seem engaged in their independent reading and responding, help the literature circle whose students may need additional support:

   * Review any of the frontloading activities as needed.

   * Address any other critical skills more appropriate for this group.

   * Assist the students with the reading of the text. Since they should have been assigned an appropriate text, encourage them to read on their own orally or silently as much as possible.

   * Provide support in completing the response activity including additional modeling and guided practice as needed.

   * Be intentional about identifying at least part of the response activity that the students would complete on their own.

   * Prepare the students to share what they have learned with the whole class since the other groups have not read their text.

Extending

1. If the members of literature circles have been reading and responding separately, invite them to share within their group what they have read and how they responded.

2. Once members have shared within their group, bring all the literature circles back together in the large group. Invite a reporter from each group to share the response to their specific text. Encourage students to make connections across texts.

3. Have students return to their literature circles and ask them to complete an informal group evaluation. Have the members discuss something that went well in their group and something that they could improve on next time. Talk about these in the large-group setting.

Illustration of a Primary Lesson

As the school year begins, Jeff falls into his familiar routine of assessing each first grader in his class to determine their strengths and needs in several aspects of early literacy (e.g., print concepts, phonological awareness, story sense, alphabetic principle, and sight word identification). He will use the information he gleans from these assessments to guide his instruction in the coming weeks.

It comes as no surprise to Jeff that he has quite a range of readers, even though this is only first grade. He has been teaching first grade for eight years now, and every year he has seen this range. This year proves no different. For example, as a result of assessing students on letter identification, he recognizes that not only are some of his students able to identify the letters of the alphabet but they are also able to read simple alphabet books. Other students can identify some of the letters whereas still others can identify few.

Using what he knows from the results of the letter identification assessment, Jeff decides to help all students understand that a main purpose for knowing letters of the alphabet is to enable their reading. He wants *all* learners to see from the onset that they can use what they know to read real books. To create this meaningful application of learning letters, Jeff decides to gather some alphabet books of varying levels that he can easily match to his students. Because he only has one copy of each book, he will group the students by mixed achievement. He will then assign specific books to particular students within each group so that each student is matched with a text that will enable successful reading. (See Jeff's lesson plan in Figure 5–3; a blank Connected Literature Circles Lesson Plan form can be found in Appendix B.)

Frontloading

Jeff opens the lesson by gathering his students into the class meeting area. Prior to the group meeting, he has gathered and displayed several objects that begin with the letter *a*. He asks students to look at the objects to see if they can figure out what they have in common. "Once you think you know, turn to your neighbor and whisper your answer." After students are finished sharing with one another, he asks for volunteers to state their thoughts. When he hears someone state that they all begin with *a*, he holds up the plastic letter *a* saying, "Exactly!"

Take note of Jeff's deliberate use of objects as opposed to just pictures. Variations of presenting information, and having students collaborate together to make conclusions about such information are powerful ways Jeff differentiated his instruction and engaged his young students.

Figure 5–3 *Jeff's ABC Lesson Plan*

Content Area: Language Arts (Reading) **Content Objective:** To identify and name objects associated with letters of the alphabet. **Comprehension Objective:** To recall details.	
Texts	1. *ABC Disney: An Alphabet Pop-Up* (Robert Sabuda 1998). New York: Disney. ISBN: 0786831324. 2. *ABC Pop!* (Rachel Isadora 1999). New York: Penguin. ISBN: 0670883298. 3. *A B C Book* (C. B. Falls 1998). New York: Morrow. ISBN: 0688147127. 4. *The Accidental Zucchini: An Unexpected Alphabet* (Max Grover 1993). San Diego, CA: Harcourt. ISBN: 0152015450. 5. *A Is for Amos* (Deborah Chandra 1999). New York: Farrar, Straus & Giroux. ISBN: 0374300011. 6. *Alice and Aldo* (Alison Lester 1996). Boston: Houghton Mifflin. ISBN: 0395870925. 7. *The Animal ABC* (Leslie Baker 2003). New York: Holt. ISBN: 0805067469.
Frontloading (Before Reading) • **Whole Class**	1. Gather the class together in the whole-group meeting area. 2. Display objects associated with the letter *a* saying something like, "Look to see what the objects have in common." After talking, show plastic letter *a*. 3. Show the children the brown bag that contains the remaining letters. Choose another letter from the bag and ask students to look around the room to see if they can spy any objects that begin with the letter. 4. Have students share a discovery with their neighbor. 5. Ask for volunteers to share what they discovered. As they share, create a semantic map on the board for all to see. Put the letter in the center and as they share, write their responses around the center drawing a line from the word to the defined center to show connections. 6. As you are writing, point out to students that you are writing the word that goes with the name of the object. 7. Once finished, have students who need additional practice in identifying letters come to the board and trace over the letter that matches the one in the defined center. 8. Show *ABC Disney* and after discussion of Disney characters, turn to the *m* page and show them the character associated with *m*. Repeat the process for another letter you draw from the bag. 9. Set the purpose for today's reading by saying something such as, "Today you will be finding a lot of objects that go with each letter of the alphabet. When you come to read with me, I'll have an alphabet book for you to read so that you can discover the objects in your book. All of you will be reading a different book when you come to the group, so let me show you the books we'll be using."

Figure 5–3 *Continued*

Frontloading (Before Reading) • **Whole Class**	10. Provide a brief overview of each alphabet book that will be used during reading. Tell students that you have selected who will read the different books and that they will discover which one they get to read when it is their turn to read with you.

Reading and Responding (During Reading)
 	
• **Mixed Achievement Groups**
	1. Call groups of five to read and respond with you in small groups while the rest work independently at centers.
	
	2. Once at the table, explain the procedure for reading their books:
	  • Read to yourselves.
	  • Look for specific objects that go with each letter of the alphabet.
	  • Reread your book if you finish before I call you together as a small group.
	  • Be ready to talk about your book when all are finished reading.
	
	3. As students read, provide help as needed. Even though you have matched readers to texts, there may still be students who need additional support reading words related to the objects shown in their books.

Extending (After Reading)
 	
• **Small Mixed Achievement Groups**
 	
• **Whole Class**
	1. Once all have finished reading, select a letter from the bag that you used with the whole class.
	
	2. Ask each student to turn to the page that shows the letter and, in turn, to state the object(s) in their books that correspond to the letter.
	
	3. In turn, invite each student to lead the group by following your example:
	  • Select a letter from the bag.
	  • Provide time for group members to locate the page in their books that show the letter and the object(s) associated with it.
	  • Ask each group member to report out.
	
	4. Once all groups have rotated to you and all have read their assigned books, gather the class together.
	
	5. Explain to the group that they will be making a class alphabet book.
	
	6. Brainstorm a topic.
	
	7. Strategically assign each child a page that represents a letter, giving students who need additional practice with a letter that specific page.
	
	8. Provide time for students to locate pictures of objects associated with their letter and to affix them on their page. Students also need to write the name of the various objects they locate.
	
	9. Assemble completed pages into an alphabet book and read it to the class.
	
	10. Display the class book in the class library for all to reread.

Jeff continues by showing students a brown paper lunch bag in which he has placed the remaining plastic letters. He shakes it saying, "I have placed plastic letters of our alphabet in this bag. I'm going to reach in, feel for one, take a guess about what it is after feeling it, and then pull it out of the bag to see if I am correct." Jeff then does just that and pulls out an *m*. He then asks students to take a look around the room to see if they can spy any objects that begin with *m* and asks them to share what they discover with their neighbor. Once students have finished sharing, Jeff asks for volunteers to state an object, writing each on the board as it is stated. He displays their responses in a semantic map, using *m* as the defined center. He comments, "I am writing the word for the objects you name. So now we have two ways of identifying the object. We can see the object itself, or a picture of it, and we can see the word that we use to label the object." Words displayed, Jeff strategically calls on volunteers to come to the board and trace over an *m* when they see one. Getting first graders to volunteer to write on the board is never a problem so without students knowing, he will be able to choose volunteers who need additional practice with identifying the letter first.

> *Capitalizing on young students' curiosity and desire to learn through play, Jeff has captivated his learners as he addresses phonics with a bit of mystery and the use of the classroom environment. In addition, ELLs have an excellent opportunity to both acquire language (naming of objects) and demonstrate their knowledge in ways not dependent on proficient use of English.*

Finally, Jeff shows the children *ABC Disney* (Sabuda 1998). He selected this book because he knows that many of his students are familiar with Disney characters. Students will be able to use their background knowledge and what they know about letters to identify the characters in the text. After reading the title, he tells students that in this ABC book, the author

> *The kinesthetic input of tracing the letter on the board is one of many ways Jeff has continued to engage his students, and include various ways of presenting information.*

shows a Disney character for every letter of the alphabet. To capitalize on what students already know about Disney characters, he tells students to partner-share a Disney character they know and calls on a few volunteers to state their ideas to the whole group. The lesson continues with Jeff stating, "I wonder what Disney character will have an *m* to start its name. Let's find out." He turns to the page that shows the *m* flap saying, "Here's the letter *m*, now I wonder what's behind the door?" Students carefully watch as Jeff slowly opens the flap. To students' delight, *Mulan* pops up. Jeff points to the printed name and says, "There's her name! So now we can recognize her in print and as a movie character!"

"Do it again!" a student requests. Using this request as an opportunity to get the students even more involved, Jeff asks a student to reach into the bag, feel for a letter, take a guess of what it is, and then take it from the bag for all to see. Once drawn from the bag, he follows the familiar routine of turning to the page that shows the letter, opening the flap, and reading the name of the character, pointing to the word while saying the name. He repeats the process a few more times and then stops, telling students that he thinks they are now ready to read their own alphabet books. Jeff comments, "Today you will be finding a lot of objects that go with each letter of the alphabet like we just did with this book. When you come to read with me, I'll have an alphabet book for you to read so that you can discover the objects in your book. All of you will be reading a different book when you come to the group, so let me show you the books we'll be using." He provides a brief preview of each book but is quick to tell students that he has decided which students will be reading which book. "It's like a surprise! You'll find out which one you get to read when you visit me for reading today!"

Reading and Responding

Jeff has a chart in the room that shows students which centers they will visit and when. His guided reading center is on this chart so students understand that they will be doing several activities that day in addition to reading. Jeff has already established the routines that will enable independent learning while away from him. He has strategically placed students' names on the chart so that students are in mixed achievement groups. When they rotate to him, he will present each person in the group with a book that is matched to their current reading level. He follows the same routine when each group comes to the reading center. First, he reminds students that they will be learning more about the alphabet by reading ABC books that contain different objects. He then comments, "I thought about each of you as I selected the books we'll be reading today. I think you'll like the book I chose just for you." Before he

Aside from the obvious differentiation within the levels of the books, Jeff has also attended to learners' needs in his structuring of the group's time. Requiring students to read to themselves, getting assistance when needed, and then preparing to talk about the text helps readers stay motivated and challenged, yet supported.

distributes the books, he sets the expectations stating, "Here's how you need to read today:

■ Read to yourselves.

■ Look for specific objects that go with each letter of the alphabet.

■ Reread your book if you finish before I call you back together as a small group.

■ Be ready to talk about your book when all are finished reading."

Jeff then distributes the books and provides students time to read them. As students read, he provides help as needed. One of the advantages of grouping students this way is that Jeff will be able to help students who need it the most while the others are meaningfully engaged. He can focus his instruction to those who need it most while at the same time providing challenging material for all students in the group.

Extending

Jeff has a couple of ideas in mind for extending the reading. For now, he will concentrate on the small group to provide some additional practice with letter identification in meaningful contexts. Once students are finished reading, he returns to the brown bag used earlier to scaffold students' reading and responding. As with the reading and responding part of the lesson, Jeff follows the same process with all groups. He begins by stating, "Now that you have finished reading, we're going to use the brown bag with letters just like we did earlier today only this time there will probably be more than one object that begins with the letter because you each read a different book." He models the process by drawing out a letter, naming it, and then asking students to turn to the page in their book that shows the letter and, in turn, to state the object(s) that correspond to the letter.

Jeff continues this process but levels the playing field by making each child the teacher. He does this by inviting each student to lead the group by following his example:

■ Select a letter from the bag.

■ Provide time for group members to locate the page in their books that shows the letter and the object(s) associated with it.

■ Ask each group member to report out.

Assigning students responsibilities usually upheld by the teacher is an outstanding way that Jeff keeps these young students engaged. In addition, once again, ELLs are provided further opportunities to increase language skills as they identify objects in their own books (and others') and match the spoken, written, and pictorial representations of a single word.

Once all groups have gone through this cycle, Jeff will have the class make their own alphabet book. As a class, they will first identify a topic. He will then assign pages to class members to either illustrate or locate pictures that correlate to their letter. With his assistance, students will label their pictures. Once all pages are finished, Jeff will assemble them into a class alphabet book, read it to them, and then place it in the class library for students to read independently.

Illustration of an Intermediate Grade Lesson

Erin has always enjoyed teaching the westward expansion theme in the fourth-grade social studies curriculum but has been a bit disappointed by the textbook presentation of this time period. While the text is clearly information rich, it lacks the personal stories that she believes more actively engage her students in historical material. She is convinced that by linking this social studies theme to her reading block, she can provide her students with access to stories that provide a rich context for both addressing key comprehension strategies and big ideas from her social studies curriculum.

Erin knows that her group of fourth graders represents a variety of reading levels. She'll not only need some grade-appropriate texts, but also a more accessible text for her readers who struggle a bit and a more challenging text for her strongest readers. She is lucky to work at a school where time and energy has been invested in securing and organizing text sets for teachers to use. She finds multiple copies of four different texts with connections to the westward expansion and pioneer life. She knows that with support the Newbery award–winning book *Sarah Plain and Tall* by Sarah MacLachlan could be handled by even her struggling readers. *Caddie Woodlawn* by Carol Ryrie Brink offers the challenge some of her stronger readers will need. Two other titles seem grade appropriate and could lend themselves for use with two other groups. The first is a novel by Gloria Whelan called *The Wanigan* about a pioneer family involved in the logging trade. The other was actually a biography called *The Story of Laura Ingalls Wilder, Pioneer Girl* by Megan Stine, which detailed the pioneer life of the author. With her text sets ready, Erin forms four literature circles of similar achievement students and assigns each text to an appropriate group. (For Erin's lesson plan, see Figure 5–4 and her groupings in Figure 5–5.) She begins to identify key strategies on which she needs to focus to strengthen the comprehension of her students. She decides on strategies that will transcend the four texts. She intentionally focuses on making connections (text-to-self connections, text-to-text connections, text-to-world connections) and promoting compare/contrast thinking patterns. She knows that focusing on these strategies will also help her students reach a deeper understanding of challenges of pioneer life.

It's important to note that although Erin does make a very conscientious effort to provide texts at appropriate levels for her students, she also is aware that students will continue to need varied levels of support as they read the chosen texts. This support will ensure that students remain engaged and challenged, as well as successful throughout the lesson.

Frontloading

Erin has decided to encourage her students to make connections and use compare and contrast thinking to reflect on the differences and similarities in pioneer family life and modern family life. She begins by sharing a personal anecdote about how her parents used to talk about things they had to do as children that had been made easier by modern conveniences for her as a child. Then she talked about things she had to do as a child that her sons would not have to do as chores because of even more modern conveniences. Erin said that she would like all the literature circles to think about this as they read their books together for this lesson. She made a chart on the board and asked the students to replicate her work in their response journals. She wrote one higher-level question at the top of the chart: *How are your family responsibilities the same as or different from the pioneer family in your book?* Then she drew two columns—one labeled *My Answer*; the other labeled *From the Book*. The students knew that in the first column they should use their own words and in the second column they should select a quote from the book to support their comment. They were also asked to add the page number of the book quote so they could refer others to it. (See Figure 5–6.)

Notice the visual and oral explanation, supported by demonstration used in the frontloading of this lesson. Erin recognizes the need to provide multiple methods of presentation, while at the same time adding to the background knowledge of the content (pioneer life). This additional background knowledge is useful to all, but essential to ELLs in Erin's class.

Content Area: Social Studies **Content Objective:** To describe experiences related to westward expansion using compare/contrast thinking patterns. **Comprehension Objective:** To practice making connections at all three levels: text to self, text to text, and text to world.	
Texts	1. *Sarah Plain and Tall* (Sarah MacLachlan 2004). New York: Scholastic. ISBN: 0590974092. 2. *Caddie Woodlawn* (Carol Ryrie Brink 2007). New York: Aladdin. ISBN: 141694818X. 3. *The Wanigan: A Life on the River* (Gloria Whelan 2002). New York: Knopf. ISBN: 0375814299. 4. *The Story of Laura Ingalls Wilder, Pioneer Girl* (Megan Stine 1992). New York: Yearling. ISBN: 0040405785.
Frontloading (Before Reading) • **Whole Class**	1. Share personal anecdote about parents talking about past childhood life compared to now with modern conveniences. 2. Tell about something you did as a child that your children will not have to do because of modern conveniences that now exist. 3. Tell students that regardless of the book they will be reading, they need to think about what the characters experience that they wouldn't have to now due to modern conveniences. 4. Draw a T-chart on the board and have students make a copy of it in their literature response journals. At the top write, *How are your family responsibilities the same as or different from the pioneer family in your book?* At the top of the column to the left, write "My Answer" and "From the Book" on the right side. (See Figure 5–6.) 5. Remind students that in the first column, they need to use their own words and in the second column they need to select and write a quote from the book including page number that supports their comment. 6. Use *When I Was Young in the Mountains* to model compare/contrast thinking to make personal and world connections. 7. Record two examples on the T-chart to show students how to complete the responding activity. 8. Continue reading aloud after reminding students to listen for additional connections. 9. After reading two pages, stop and ask volunteers to add to the class chart. 10. Refer children to the chart that shows their names and the title the group will read. (See Figure 5–5.)

(continues)

Figure 5–4 *Continued*

Reading and Responding (During Reading) • **Groups**	1. Provide time for students to group themselves according to the chart. 2. Provide guidelines for completing the reading and responding activities and set a deadline for when both need to be finished. 3. Remind students of their options for when they are finished with the day's reading and responding: read other related texts about pioneer life that are displayed in the classroom library. 4. Reminders in place, provide time for students to read in their groups while you monitor. Land on the group that will need additional support to read and respond to the text.
Extending (After Reading)	1. Reconvene the entire class. 2. Display the three-column chart large enough for all to see: *Title, Pioneer Family Responsibilities, Modern Family Responsibilities*. (See Figure 5–7.) 3. Ask for a volunteer from each group to take on the role of reporter and report to the rest of the class differences and similarities between pioneer family responsibilities and modern family responsibilities. 4. Add reporter's responses to the chart next to the corresponding title. 5. After all groups have had time to add to the chart, ask for other volunteers to add additional information. 6. Remind students that they can add additional pertinent information to the chart when they are reading independently. 7. Provide time for students to complete a group evaluation related to their interaction with one another for today.

Using *When I Was Young in the Mountains,* a picture book by Cynthia Rylant (2002), Erin read aloud from the book, paused when appropriate and did a think-aloud to show compare and contrast thinking in making personal and world connections. She recorded a few examples on the chart to review how to complete the response activity. She read further in the book and asked students to listen for additional connections. Erin paused and prompted her students to help her add to the chart. Once the students seemed ready to work away from her, Erin pointed to the chart indicating the members of each literature circle and guided them as they moved to begin their work together.

Figure 5–5 *Connected Literature Circle Groups*

Accessible Text: *Sarah Plain and Tall*	Easier Grade-Level Text: *The Story of Laura Ingalls Wilder, Pioneer Girl*	Harder Grade-Level Text: *The Wanigan*	Challenge Text: *Caddie Woodlawn*
1.	1.	1.	1.
2.	2.	2.	2.
3.	3.	3.	3.
4.	4.	4.	4.
5.	5.	5.	5.
6.	6.	6.	6.

Figure 5–6 *T-Chart for Literature Response Journal*

How are your family responsibilities the same as or different from the pioneer family in your book?	
My Answer	**From the Book**

Reading and Responding

Erin reached the point in the lesson where she was ready to turn the reading and response activities over to her literature circles. She instructs her groups to continue reading their pioneer life books responding to the key question about family responsibilities for their specific text. She allows the members of each literature circle to define how they will move forward with the reading and response for the titles they are reading but sets a deadline for when the work must be done. She reminds the students of their rules for doing work in literature circles and what they can do when they are all done with their work including continuing to read in their texts or in any of the related texts about pioneer life available in the room. She monitors the literature circles as they get engaged with their task. She knows that two of the groups have the ability to work together without much intervention, so she moves her chair next to the circle that she knows will need the most support. She keeps an eye on the nearby group who sometimes needs a little direction from her as well, but she starts with the group who she knows will need the most support. It's her *Sarah Plain and Tall* group. She helps them get some momentum in reading the next section of the book and a good start on completing the response activity. She wants to make sure that they have enough support to finish the chapter on their own and feel confident sharing their responses with others in the class. This allows her some direct contact time with the Laura Ingalls group. She double-checks to see if they have made progress in their reading and response. She provides enough support to help them reach closure on their chapter and the response. Erin quickly checks to see if *The Wanigan* and the *Caddie Woodlawn* groups are close to finishing. They give her a thumbs-up sign.

> The differentiation provided in Erin's support of these groups, possibly by reading portions of the text aloud, scaffolding questions to elicit students' connections to the text, and/or even providing assistance in the writing of responses, will create multiple opportunities for success, keep students engaged, and provide various ways for students to demonstrate their knowledge through discussion and writing.

Extending

Erin brings all the literature circles back together. In the front of the room, she has created a chart with three columns: *Title, Pioneer Family Responsibilities, Modern Family Responsibilities*. (See Figure 5–7.) She strategically selects a reporter from each literature circle. She starts with her *Sarah Plain and Tall* group. The reporter shares the results of their group's response activity identi-

Figure 5–7 *Group Chart Across Text Response*   **87**

How are your family responsibilities the same as or different from the pioneer family in your book?		
Title	Pioneer Family Responsibilities	Modern Family Responsibilities
Sarah Plain and Tall		
The Story of Laura Ingalls Wilder, Pioneer Girl		
The Wanigan		
Caddie Woodlawn		

fying the differences and similarities between pioneer family responsibilities and modern family responsibilities. These are added to the chart for that title. Similar reporting is done by reporters for each of the other titles. After all responses are recorded, Erin calls on some additional voices to help find some key insights between pioneer families and modern families. These are added as a way of summarizing what has been learned. She invites students reading other related titles and examples to add to the chart during independent work time. After the follow-up activity, Erin has each literature circle meet briefly to do a group evaluation on their work together for the day. She checks with each group and talks about what students thought they did well and what they might improve on for next time.

Erin's strategic selection of a reporter from each literature circle exemplifies Erin's knowledge of her students' individual strengths. Therefore, students having strong expressive language skills have a chance to shine, while the rest of the class benefits from the opportunity to hear information presented by someone other than the teacher.

Additional Resources

Following are some additional text sets that are suitable for first or second graders. Each set contains books of varying difficulty levels should you want to use them like Jeff used the alphabet books with his first graders.

Alphabet Titles

Title	Author	Publisher/Year ISBN
A Is for . . . ? A Photographer's Alphabet of Animals	Henry Horenstein	Harcourt/1999 0152015825
ABC Kids	Laura Williams	Philomel/2000 0399233709
Action Alphabet	Shelley Rotner	Simon & Schuster/1996 068980086X
Agent A to Agent Z	Andy Rash	Scholastic/2004 0439368820
Alphabeep: A Zipping, Zooming ABC	Deborah Pearson	Holiday House/2003 9780823420766
B Is for Big Sky Country: A Montana Alphabet	Sneed Collard III	Sleeping Bear/2003 1585360988
B Is for Bulldozer: A Construction ABC	June Sobel	Harcourt/2003 0152022503
Ellsworth's Extraordinary Electric Ears and Other Amazing Alphabet Anecdotes	Valore Fisher	Simon & Schuster/2003 0689850301
Miss Spider's ABC	David Kirk	Scholastic/1998 0590282794
The ABC Bunny	Wanda Gag	Putnam & Grosset/ 1997 0698114388

Title	Author	Publisher/Year ISBN
The Wacky Wedding: A Book of Alphabet Antics	Pamela Duncan	Hyperion/1999 0786822481
William Wegman ABC	William Wegman	Hyperion/1994 1562826964

Color Titles

Title	Author	Publisher/Year ISBN
Brown Bear, Brown Bear, What Do You See?	Bill Martin Jr.	Holt /1964 0805047905
Color Zoo	Lois Ehlert	HarperCollins/1997 0694010677
Colors	Robert Crowther	Candlewick/2001 0763614041
The Deep Blue Sea: A Book of Colors	Audrey Wood	Scholastic/2005 0439753821
I Spy Colors in Art	Lucy Micklethwait	Greenwillow/2007 9780061348372
Is It Red? Is It Yellow? Is It Blue?	Tana Hoban	Greenwillow/1978 0688801714
Who Said Red?	Mary Serfozo	Houghton Mifflin /1988 0689504551

Shape Titles

Title	Author	Publisher/Year ISBN
Circles and Squares Everywhere!	Max Grover	Harcourt/1996 0152000917
The Hole Story	Eve Merriam	Simon & Schuster/1995 0671883534

Title	Author	Publisher/Year ISBN
Sea Shapes	Suse MacDonald	Harcourt/1994 0152000275
Shape Capers	Cathryn Falwell	Greenwillow/2007 9780061237003
Shape Space	Catherine Falwell	Clarion/1992 039561305
The Shape of Things	Dale Dodds	Candlewick/1994 1564022242

The following are some additional text sets that are suitable for third to fifth graders. Each set contains books of varying difficulty levels.

Courage

Title	Author	Publisher/Year ISBN
Bright Shadow	Avi	Scholastic/2000 0689717830
Eagle Song	Joseph Bruchac	Puffin/1990 0141301694
Journey to Jo'burg	Beverly Naidoo	HarperTrophy/1988 0064402371
Night of the Twisters	Ivy Ruckman	HarperTrophy/1986 0064401766

Famous Women

Title	Author	Publisher/Year ISBN
Helen Keller	Margaret Davidson	Scholastic/1989 0590424041

Title	Author	Publisher/Year ISBN
Jane Addams: Social Worker	Charnan Simon	Children's Press/1998 0516262351
Laura Ingalls Wilder	Patricia Reilly Giff	Puffin/1988 0140320741
Walking the Road to Freedom	Jeri Ferris	Carolrhoda Books/1989 0876145055

Friendship

Title	Author	Publisher/Year ISBN
The Bully of Barkham Street	Mary Stolz	HarperCollins/1987 0064401596
The Hot and Cold Summer	Johanna Hurwitz	Scholastic/1991 0590428586
J. T.	Jane Wagner	Yearling/1972 0440442753
Nothing's Fair in Fifth Grade	Barthe DeClements	Listening Library/1991 0140344438

Humorous Stories

Title	Author	Publisher/Year ISBN
Be a Perfect Person in Just Three Days!	Stephen Manes	Yearling/1996 0440413494
Dogs Don't Tell Jokes	Louis Sachar	Yearling/1992 0679833722
My Life as a Fifth Grade Comedian	Elizabeth Levy	Scholastic/2000 0439223614
The Plant That Ate Dirty Socks	Nancy McArthur	HarperTrophy/1988 0380754932

Mystery

Title	Author	Publisher/Year ISBN
Finding Buck Henry	Alfred Slate	HarperTrophy/1992 0064404692
The Gypsy Game	Zilpha Keatley Snyder	Yearling/1998 0440412587
Return to Howliday Inn	James Howe	Aladdin/2007 1416939679
Sammy Keyes and the Skeleton Man	Wendelin Van Draanen	Scholastic/2004 0439981247

Survival

Title	Author	Publisher/Year ISBN
Hatchet	Gary Paulsen	Alladin/2006 1416936475
Julie of the Wolves	Jean Craighead George	HarperTrophy/2005 0060739444
My Side of the Mountain	Jean Craighead George	Puffin/2004 0142401110
Trouble River	Betsy Byars	Puffin/1989 0140342435

Model 4:
Focused Readers' Workshop

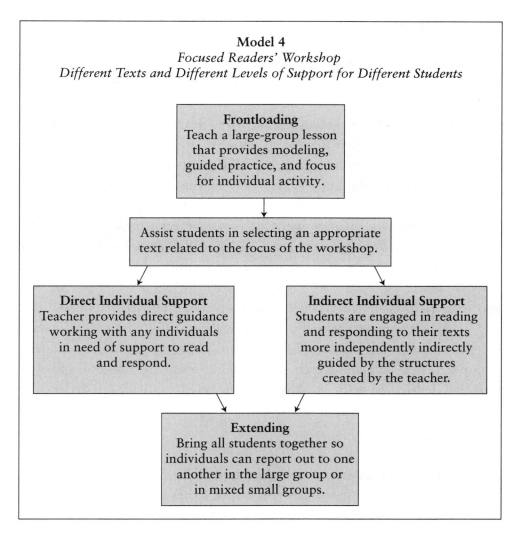

Model 4
Focused Readers' Workshop
Different Texts and Different Levels of Support for Different Students

Frontloading
Teach a large-group lesson that provides modeling, guided practice, and focus for individual activity.

Assist students in selecting an appropriate text related to the focus of the workshop.

Direct Individual Support
Teacher provides direct guidance working with any individuals in need of support to read and respond.

Indirect Individual Support
Students are engaged in reading and responding to their texts more independently indirectly guided by the structures created by the teacher.

Extending
Bring all students together so individuals can report out to one another in the large group or in mixed small groups.

Figure 6–1

Scenario

It is now January. You are pleased that your students have become increasingly more competent, confident, and comfortable with reading because all three of these characteristics are important for engendering a desire to read for a variety of purposes, both in and out of school. Their feelings of competence, confidence, and comfort reflect your deliberate attempts to instill these feelings through numerous focused lessons and using different grouping structures. Students feel like a part of the classroom community.

Recognizing that your students have made great strides in their reading abilities, you decide that it is time to let them grow even further by creating a reading environment that mirrors what readers do in their everyday lives. Readers select their own texts, set a purpose for reading, and adjust their reading rate to coincide with their purpose for reading. They also choose different ways of responding to the text. Sometimes, readers respond while they read. Some make notations in the margins. Others stop reading, mentally reflect, and then continue reading without writing any comments. And there are others who just need to stop and talk about what they are reading with someone else.

As much as you want your students to learn these most important attributes, you realize that this means allowing student choice to play a significant role in your reading program. This means moving toward a more individualized approach. But you get a little nervous trying to figure out how you will be able to manage everything. How do you keep a handle on the growth of individual readers while at the same time targeting necessary instruction that will help them maximize their full potential as readers? You decide that you might be able to manage this instruction by using a focused readers' workshop model (see Figure 6–1). It provides a safety net for you and your students alike. It will help you to open up students' reading options and provide a common thread that you will use to build an instructional focus throughout the workshop simultaneously. You will be able to differentiate instruction by helping each student select a just-right text and further differentiate by varying the levels of support you will provide for students.

Explanation

Like literature circles, readers' workshop approaches have been implemented by different teachers in many different forms. In her now classic text, *In the Middle* (1987), Nancie Atwell brought forth the idea of readers' workshop.

She has since reenergized this charge in her most recent book, *The Reading Zone* (2007). Working initially with middle schoolers, Atwell argues for a workshop format that emulates more of a studio atmosphere. In essence, her readers' workshop is based on the idea that students learn to read by reading and that certain conditions must be in place in order for the workshop to work best for all including

- silent reading

- reading or responding to reading the entire workshop time

- updating reading logs

- reading independently when the teacher is conferencing with a fellow classmate

In Atwell's vision, students control their choices of texts and responses. Students are allowed to move at their own pace, which often means that students are at different points in the process just like artists working in a studio.

On the other end of the continuum, some educators argue for a workshop format that is a bit tighter in its flow with teachers taking control of some aspects of the process. For example, Reutzel and Cooter's (1991, 2008) version of readers' workshop lasts for seventy minutes and includes five components: (1) a five- to ten-minute sharing time, during which time the teacher shares new text discoveries as a way to ignite interest in reading; (2) a five- to ten-minute minilesson (i.e., a short, whole-group instructional session in which the teacher demonstrates something that the students need to know about reading); (3) a five-minute state of the class, a chart that shows where students are in their reading and is used to document progress; (4) ten-minute self-selected reading and a fifteen- to twenty-minute response, which calls on students to read and respond to a self-selected text; and (5) a five- to ten-minute sharing time when the whole class comes together to share reading discoveries during the workshop. This more prescriptive format tightens the instruction provided during the workshop.

The focused readers' workshop we explain and describe in this chapter (see Figure 6–2) shares many of the characteristics common to Atwell and Reutzel and Cooter. For instance, it typically starts with a whole-class, teacher-directed focus lesson that aims to guide students as they independently read and respond to their individual texts. These lessons evolve from the assessed needs of the students and the demands of the local curriculum.

Figure 6–2 *Key Elements of Focused Readers' Workshop*

Key Elements	Focused Readers' Workshop Model
Text	Different but related texts for every student. Effort is made to make sure the text collection contains enough levels to match those of the students and have the capability of providing targeted connections across the texts.
Grouping	Begin with the whole class for the focused lesson and response activity that all will complete. Progress to individual silent reading and responding to the text. Regroup with the whole class to debrief the readers' workshop for the day. Students may work with partners and teams for some workshop activities.
Differentiation	Assign predetermined related texts to better match the performance levels of each student. You might also want to consider grouping books at a given level and having students select from among those texts. Another way to differentiate is to provide varying levels of support to students as needed.
Best Uses	This model works best when a wide variety of connected texts of various levels are available for all learners in the classroom community to collaboratively explore a common topic, theme, genre, author, literary element, or comprehension strategy.
Advantages	• It builds community across the classroom by providing shared experiences while matching students with texts more appropriate to their reading levels. • It uses real texts in a setting that more closely mirrors what readers do in their everyday lives. • It allows for the greatest match of individual texts with individual students to better address what might have the greatest attraction for individual students.
Disadvantages	• The teacher needs access to and knowledge of multiple texts written at various reading levels that can still provide an opportunity for connected conversations across the classroom community. • The teacher needs to take time to teach students how to read and respond independently so that they will stay engaged as strategic readers. (See Chapter 7 for specific ideas and Appendix A for more resources.)

They are intentionally designed to target instruction around critical process and content outcomes needed by most students in the class. Following the lesson, time is set aside for all readers to read individual books, reading at their own pace staying focused on comprehension. After a specified silent reading period elapses, all readers respond to their texts in a manner that relates to the day's focus lesson. You use open-ended response activities that transcend reading levels so that all readers have something to contribute when the class comes back together.

Conferencing is an integral part of the focused readers' workshop. During this time, the teacher meets with individual students or small groups of individuals to support their efforts as needed and to assess their progress. Most often this conferencing time happens while others are silently reading and/or responding.

The focused readers' workshop concludes with a community sharing time. The teacher reconvenes the whole class and systematically invites students to share with others their discoveries related to the assigned response activity. When time allows, the sharing time may also provide an opportunity to talk beyond the specific response activity. That is, students might want to share other discoveries and show others the books they are reading.

One of the primary differences in the focused workshop is that it retains an element of teacher control and limits student choice. If the model is to provide differentiated instruction, then it might be better to have students choose from a collection of predetermined texts that the teacher selects to better ensure it matches with students' performance levels. Students will still self-select a text but within a range of choices.

Another way control and choice are balanced thereby allowing for more effective differentiation is by securing a collection of texts that is related in some manner. Texts with potential connections allow for more manageable classroom conversations to occur across texts. We might, like Carol in the primary grade example shown on page 101, have students choose from among an array of animal texts so that readers' workshop can serve as a catalyst for reading about a science-related topic to discover specific information set forth in the whole-group minilesson. Targeting key language and content outcomes through these connections tightens up the workshop to make sure readers are addressing critical strategies and ideas.

While the implementation of a workshop approach that clearly individualizes instruction may be the best vehicle for differentiating instruction, complete student choice may not mean that all students receive the instruction that targets critical strategies and content. Students may not always choose to work on what they need to work on or what the curriculum suggests they should work on. Masterful teachers may lead students to those choices, but would that be the most efficient use of teaching time? For effective differentiation, we may need to be more intentional as we focus readers either collectively or individually. We also want to suggest that a workshop approach that moves closer to the goal of individualized differentiated instruction is probably a lot easier to implement if we have had a successful experience with focused workshop approaches first.

General Teaching Suggestions

Preparation

1. Select texts with a significant common element that are written at multiple levels to match the readers in the classroom.

2. Plan prereading activities that will transcend the titles but connect the conversations across them. Focus on strategies defined by local standards and needed by the students as revealed in ongoing assessments.

3. Carefully consider how to match texts to individual students.

4. Plan response activities that will engage students as they work independently.

5. Be prepared to provide support to any individual or group of individuals that may require additional teacher guidance.

6. Set up a structure to conference with individuals to assess whether standards are being met.

7. Plan extension activities that bring the class together as a community of learners and leads to conversations across and beyond the texts.

Frontloading

1. If appropriate, teach the focus lesson by using a personal example from your life.

2. Invite students to provide examples from their own lives that also illustrate the focus lesson.

3. Read aloud a short text or text selection that models the focus lesson within a text. As you are reading, model how to do the response activity. As appropriate, have the students replicate your work.

4. Invite all students to turn to their own texts and see if they can surface more examples to illustrate the focus lesson. As they are reading on their own, monitor to see that they can do the response activity without you.

5. Set a clear purpose for continuing the reading and responding to individual texts.

6. State visible written directions for independent work.

Reading and Responding

1. Turn the completion of the task modeled and practiced during the frontloading over to the students:

   * Review the directions as needed.

   * Review any class rules as needed about working independently.

   * Clearly identify one or two activities that the students can do when they are finished reading and responding if other students are still working. Encourage students to continue reading in their own texts or read any additional texts that are available in the classroom.

   * Get students started on the reading and response activity.

2. Once individuals are engaged in their independent reading and responding, begin conferencing with individual students especially those in need of additional support. During the conference:

   * Review any of the frontloading activities as needed.

   * Address any other critical skills more appropriate for this individual student.

   * Monitor the student's ability to read the text.

   * Monitor the student's ability to complete the response activity providing support as needed.

   * Prepare the student to be able to contribute to the extension activity with a partner, small group, or with the whole class.

Extending

1. Each student will need to work with other students as partners, in small groups, or in the large group as they begin to make connections across texts related to the instructional focus.

2. Bring all students together. Set up a community sharing forum that systematically invites students to share how they completed the response activity for the book they were reading.

3. Provide some time for students to have conversations about their books across the classroom community.

4. Spend time asking the individuals to complete self-evaluations. Have the students reflect on something that they did well and something that they could improve on next time. Talk about these in the large-group setting.

Illustration of a Primary Lesson

Carol's second graders have been learning about animals in science. To extend their understanding of likenesses and differences among animals and to give students some practice reading nonfiction, she decides that she will fold learning about animals into the focused readers' workshop. She has used it with these students on other occasions and her students are familiar with the accompanying routines.

To prepare for the workshop, she will gather texts that represent students' instructional reading levels and will display them on one of three tables. (See the Additional Resources at the end of the chapter for a suggested list of animal texts.) She will number each table with a 1, 2, or 3 and display a range of texts that reflects the students who will be instructed to go to that table to self-select a book. Rather than call attention to reading level, Carol will give students a number (either 1, 2, or 3) as they walk into the classroom. She will explain to students that when they self-select their books that they must do so from the table that corresponds to their number. Figure 6–3 shows Carol's three-part, focused workshop lesson plan. (A blank Focused Readers' Workshop Lesson Plan form can be found in Appendix B.)

Frontloading

Carol begins the lesson with the whole class with a read-aloud, *The Big Book of Animals* (Hanly 1997). Once finished, Carol has students think about an animal mentioned in the text and where that animal might live. She then has them share their thoughts with the person sitting near them. Finally, she asks for volunteers to share their ideas. After each sharing, the person who shared must locate the page(s) in the text that supports his or her answer. Carol then comments, "As you can see, every animal lives in a certain place. This place is called *habitat*." She writes the word on the righthand side of a two-column chart she has created.

Carol's use of the think-pair-share method is a powerful way for ELLs (and others) to feel confident about participating within whole-group discussions.

Figure 6–3 *Carol's Focused Workshop Lesson Plan*   **101**

Content Area: Science **Content Objective:** To identify how all animals are alike by identifying their unique habitats. **Comprehension Objective:** To read about given animals and locate information about their habitats.	
Texts	• Read aloud: *The Big Book of Animals* (Hanly 1997). ISBN: 0789414856. • See the Additional Resources at the end of the chapter for a listing of animal texts.
Frontloading (Before Reading) • **Whole Class**	1. Gather the class together in the meeting area. 2. Ask students to think about an animal they know about and where it lives. 3. Introduce the read-aloud by reading the title and asking students to listen to learn if their animal is mentioned. 4. Read aloud *The Big Book of Animals.* 5. Provide time for students to talk with a partner about an animal mentioned in the story and where it lives. Students can also talk about whether their animal was mentioned. 6. Ask for volunteers to share an animal they heard mentioned in the story and where it lives. 7. Locate page(s) in the text that supports the response. 8. Explain the meaning of *habitat.* 9. Create a two-column chart. 10. Tell students that they will be completing the class chart when they have finished reading in readers' workshop.
Reading and Responding (During Reading) • **Individuals**	1. Explain reading procedures for the twenty-minute reading period using the class chart. (Refer to Figure 6–4.) 2. Provide time for students to select books. 3. Provide time for students to read and respond to their texts. 4. Once students are reading, individually conference with students who may need more support in locating habitats for their animals.

(continues)

Figure 6–3 *Continued*

Extending (After Reading) • Triads	1. Strategically group students into triads making sure that there is a 1, 2, and 3 representative in each triad.
	2. Provide time for students to share their discoveries with one another.
	3. Tell students to select one animal and its habitat and to write each on a separate sticky note.
	4. Gather all students in the meeting area. Make sure they bring their completed sticky notes with them.
	5. In turn, have students place their sticky notes in the appropriate columns on the class chart that was shown at the start of the workshop.
	6. Leave the chart displayed so that students can add additional discoveries.

On the lefthand side of the chart, she writes *Animal*. She comments, "We have been learning about animals during science and today you are going to learn even more by reading about animals during readers' workshop."

Reading and Responding

Carol continues by explaining how they will select their books and the other procedures for the twenty-minute reading and responding time. She tells the students, "We have used readers' workshop before but today it's a little different because you will need to choose your book from a certain table." She refers them to the "Readers' Workshop Procedures" chart and reviews each step (refer to Figure 6–4).

Procedures in place, Carol provides time for students to select their books and to get settled. Once all are reading, she begins to conference with individual students beginning with those students she suspects may need more support in identifying habitats. She first checks to see that the student can read his or her text. She

Although Carol had indicated that students could write their responses in the frontloading portion of this lesson, she may further differentiate within individual conferences by encouraging students to draw pictures of the habitat and corresponding animal within the appropriate columns on their charts. This would provide the student with another option to express his or her knowledge, as well as another way for other students in the class to acquire the knowledge as the sharing session takes place.

Figure 6–4 *Readers' Workshop Procedures* **103**

Readers' Workshop Procedures

1. Select a book from the table that corresponds to the number that I gave you when you walked into the classroom.

2. Silently read your book.

3. Identify at least one animal mentioned in the book and its habitat.

4. In your reading response log, write the name of the animal and its habitat.

5. Continue reading and identifying animals and their habitats until I signal you that it is time to come together as a whole group.

---

then checks to see if the reader can find the name of an animal and identify its habitat. Finally, she checks to make sure that the student knows how to use the explained format to record the animal name and its habitat.

Extending

Approximately twenty minutes later, Carol signals to the readers that it is time to stop reading and responding. She strategically groups students into triads, making sure that each triad has a student who represents a 1, 2, and 3. She provides students time to share their discoveries with one another using their books and their response logs as reminders. As students share, Carol circulates and monitors to make sure that groups stay focused and that every student gets an opportunity to share.

After about five minutes, Carol provides each student with two sticky notes. She instructs each student to choose one animal and its habitat and to write each on a separate sticky note. She then calls the whole class together telling them to bring their sticky notes with them. Once seated, she comments, "Well, it looks to me like you were all able to find many different

Notice how Carol uses sticky notes as a tool to keep learners engaged in the lesson, to synthesize and organize the information acquired independently and in small groups, and finally to provide a resource for students to continue to contribute to each others' knowledge base beyond this lesson. Doing so provides learners with a challenge that is often very motivating for many of her students.

animals and their habitats. Let's get some of them up here." In turn, students place their sticky notes under the appropriate column on the class chart that was created at the start of the workshop. Carol closes the workshop noting, "So just like us, every animal needs a place to live, a *habitat*. This is one way that all animals are alike. You may find other animals and their habitats when you read. If so, you can add them to our chart."

Illustration of an Intermediate Grade Lesson

As part of ongoing instruction about story grammar and how the elements can assist readers and writers, Carmen wants all of her fourth-grade students to zero in on how the author provides clues to the story setting by having them attend to the author's language about setting. She believes that by doing so students will better comprehend the texts they are reading and they will also be able to better create a sense of setting in their own writing. In preparation for the lesson, she will guide each student to select a narrative text matched to each reader so that each can read the text without frustration. In this way, readers will be able to devote the majority of their energy to how the author uses language to signal the setting.

Frontloading

Carmen opens the lesson with the whole class (see her lesson plan in Figure 6–5). She places an excerpt from Paul Fleischman's *The Borning Room* (pages 3–4) on an overhead transparency so that all students can read the text. The enlarged example also allows her to show good choices made by the author to describe the sense of place, time, and mood for the story in the opening chapter of the book. Since Fleischman actually tells the reader: "Look out the window," Carmen uses that as a metaphor for what readers should do when they start a new book or the scene in the story changes. She comments, "When you start a new book or a chapter from a book, it is much like looking out a new window to take notice of what's there. The challenge is that as an author, you only get to use words to create the scene. That's why authors spend a lot of time thinking about the words they use and why they use certain words. As a reader, you know when an author has been successful in

Knowing that simply listening to Fleischman's text read aloud will not meet the needs of many of her learners, Carmen reads the text aloud while also displaying the text. This display increases students' interest while also attending to both student strengths and needs in regard to learning modalities.

Figure 6–5 *Carmen's Focused Workshop Lesson Plan*

105

	Content Area: Language Arts **Content Objective:** To identify good examples of setting language to use strategically when writing and reading. **Comprehension Objective:** To use language clues about time, place, and mood to understand the setting of a story.
Texts	• Read aloud: *The Borning Room* (Fleischman 1993). ISBN: 0064470997. • See the Additional Resources at the end of the chapter for a link to other texts with good examples of setting language.
Frontloading (Before Reading) • **Whole Class**	1. Gather the class together in the meeting area. 2. Place the transparency of the opening paragraphs from *The Borning Room* (pages 3–4) so that all students can read the text. 3. Read aloud part of the excerpt. 4. Share a think-aloud revealing the good choices made by the author to describe the sense of place, time, and mood for the story. Highlight identified language examples on the transparency. 5. Point out how the author uses similes, metaphors, and descriptive language to create sensory images readers can use to fully understand the setting for the story. Remind students that they should try to create similar images when they write. 6. Invite students to read part of the remaining text on the screen with you. Ask them to help you identify additional examples from the opening part of the book. Let students highlight those language examples on the transparency. 7. Tell the students that the task for the day is to find at least four good examples of setting language in the books they are reading. Tell them to use sticky notes to mark the examples or record them in their learning log and be ready to share examples with others at the end of the workshop.

Reading and Responding (During Reading)
 	
• **Individuals**
	1. Explain to students the expectations for today's reading time.
	2. Create a chart large enough for all to see and review each step:
	  • Silently read your text for twenty minutes.
	  • Either during or after reading use your sticky notes to indicate at least four examples of setting language.
	  • If you get finished reading and responding before others, go ahead and continue reading in your book and find additional examples of setting language.

(continues)

Figure 6–5 *Continued*

Reading and Responding (During Reading) • **Individuals**	3. As students begin to read, monitor to make sure all are engaged. 4. Begin to conference with individual students beginning with those students who may need more support in identifying setting language. Make sure the student can read his or her text. Then check to see if the reader can find examples of setting language.

Extending (After reading)
 	
• **Teams**
	1. Bring all the students back together as a group.
	
	2. Prepare a set of file folders for each team that contains one overhead transparency, one overhead pen, and the directions for the group activity.
	
	3. Review the directions:
	
	  • In turn, each team member shares the examples of setting language they found in the books they were reading.
	
	  • Once all have shared, decide which four you want to write on the overhead transparency.
	
	  • Either choose a recorder to write all of the examples, or have students take turns writing the four examples on the transparency.
	
	  • Place a star next to the one you would like to write on the class chart.
	
	4. As students work in teams, circulate providing additional support where needed.
	
	5. Once the teams have completed their transparencies, select a reporter from each group to come to the front of the classroom and share their examples on the overhead and discuss why they thought these were good examples.
	
	6. Post a large sheet of white paper for students to record their starred best sample examples of setting language.
	
	7. Leave the paper displayed and encourage students to add to the chart as they continue to find good examples in the books they are reading.

communicating what's outside the window because you have an image of it. As a writer, you know you are successful when you read your story to others and they respond just the way you had wanted them to respond." She continues by explaining that authors use language in many different ways to help convey ideas to readers. "Take a look at what this author has done," she says while pointing to specific phrases, metaphors and similes, and interesting descriptive words shown in the displayed text. "Amazing, isn't it? There's a lot to writing a story, isn't there?" She then tells students that they will be looking for the way the author uses language to help the reader get a sense of the story setting and provides students with the text they will be reading to discover this information. She tells the students that their task for the day is to find at least four good examples of setting language as they read their books. She tells them they can use their sticky notes to mark the examples or record them in their learning log, but they need to be ready to share four examples with other students when the workshop time for reading and writing is finished.

> *Carmen's decision to allow students a variety of materials (sticky notes or learning logs) to respond to their reading shows her awareness of how materials can influence both the motivation and engagement in a particular activity. Fourth graders, Carmen realizes, appreciate this acknowledgment of their maturity and ability to make responsible decisions for their learning.*

Reading and Responding

Carmen continues the lesson by explaining to students the expectations for today's twenty-minute reading time. On a chart large enough for all to see, she reviews each step saying, "Here's what you need to do during our readers' workshop time today:

1. Silently read your text for twenty minutes.

2. Either during or after reading, use your sticky notes or learning logs to indicate examples of setting language.

3. If you get finished reading and responding before others, go ahead and continue reading in your book and find additional examples of setting language. Or look in the book you are reading for independent silent reading to see if you can find a good example of setting language."

As students begin reading, Carmen monitors to make sure all students are engaged. She then begins to conference with individual students she suspects may need more support in identifying setting language. She first checks to see that the student can read his or her text. She then checks to see if the reader can find examples of setting language. Before she ends the conference, Carmen provides the student with enough practice so that he or she feels confident about sharing an example of setting language with other students.

Notice that Carmen is deliberate in her support of students' preparation to share within the whole group. This rehearsal is often the difference between risk taking and silence for many ELL students in Carmen's classroom.

Extending

Once the twenty-minute reading and responding time concludes, Carmen brings all the students back together. She comments, "Well it looks like you found some excellent examples. Here's how I would like you to share with one another." Referring to a set of file folders, she opens one so that students can see their names commenting, "You'll notice that I have put you into teams of four. This is team one. You'll also notice that in this folder there is one overhead transparency, one overhead pen, and the directions for your group activity. Let's review the directions." Holding up the directions contained in the folder, she points to each as she reads it aloud:

Within this extending section of her plan, Carmen has used a variety of materials in the multiple methods of presenting the information that she desires all students to acquire. This, paired with extensive work in small groups, supports the success of every student in her class.

1. In turn, each team member shares the examples of setting language he or she found in their reading books.

2. Once all have shared, decide which four examples you want to write on the overhead transparency.

3. Either choose a recorder to write all of the examples, or take turns writing the four examples on the transparency.

4. Place a star next to the one you would like to write on the class chart.

As students share, Carmen circulates, providing additional support as needed. Once the teams have completed their transparencies, Carmen systematically selects a reporter from each group to come to the front of the classroom to share the examples on the overhead and discuss why the group thought these were good examples. She then posts a large sheet of white paper for students to record their starred examples of setting language. Carmen leaves the paper displayed and encourages all readers to add to the chart as they continue to find good examples in the books they are reading on succeeding days. She then provides time for the team to evaluate their work together for the lesson and share their insights in the large group.

Additional Resources

Animal Texts for Carol's Focused Workshop

Title	Author	Publisher/Year ISBN
All About Turtles	Jim Arnosky	Scholastic/2000 0590481495
Amazing Spiders	Alexandra Parsons	Dorling Kindersley/1990 0863184316
Animals Black and White	Phyllis Limbacher Tildes	Charlesbridge/1996 0881069590
Ape	Martin Jenkins	Candlewick/2007 9780763634711
Bald Eagle	Gordon Morrison	Houghton Mifflin/2003 0618386262
Beaver	Glen Rounds	Holiday House/1999 082341440X
The Big Book of Animals	Shiela Hanly	DK/1997 9780789414854
Castles, Caves, and Honeycombs	Linda Ashman	Harcourt/2001 0152022112

Title	Author	Publisher/Year ISBN
Chameleon, Chameleon	Joy Cowley	Scholastic/2005 0439666538
Cow	Malachy Doyle	Simon & Schuster/2002 068984462X
Crocodiles and Alligators	Seymour Simon	HarperCollins/1999 0060274743
Crows! Strange and Wonderful	Laurence Pringle	Boyds Mills/2002 1563978997
Ducks!	Gail Gibbons	Holiday House/2001 0823415678
Frogs	James Martin	Crown/1997 0517709058
Gentle Giant Octopus	Karen Wallace	Candlewick/1998 076361730X
Growing Up Wild: Wolves	Sandra Markle	Simon & Schuster/2001 0689818866
Growing Up Wild: Bears	Sandra Markle	Simon & Schuster/2000 0689818882
Hello, Fish! Visiting the Coral Reef	Sylvia Earle	National Geographic/2001 0792266978
Here Is the Wetland	Madeleine Dunphy	Hyperion/1996 0786801646
Jaguar in the Rainforest	Joanne Ryder	Morrow/1996 0688129900
A Manatee Morning	Jim Arnosky	Simon & Schuster/2000 0689816049
Owls	Gail Gibbons	Holiday House/2005 0823418804
Pigs	Gail Gibbons	Holiday House/1999 0823414418
Penguins	Seymour Simon	Smithsonian/Collins/2007 9780060283964

Title	Author	Publisher/Year ISBN
Slinky Scaly Slithery Snakes	Dorothy Hinshaw Patent	Walker/2000 0802787436
Snakes Biggest! Littlest!	Sandra Markle	Boyds Mills/2005 1590781899
South American Animals	Caroline Arnold	Morrow/1999 0688155642
Surprising Sharks	Nicola Davies	Candlewick/2003 0763621854
Tracks in the Wild	Betsy Bowen	Houghton Mifflin/1999 0395884004
Wild Flamingos	Bruce McMillan	Houghton Mifflin/1997 0395845459

Link for Bibliographies of Books to Use in Teaching Setting

www.readwritethink.org/lesson_images/lesson107/SettingBooklist.pdf

7

Yeah . . . But . . . What About These Questions?

As a result of our teaching and consulting experiences, we have had several opportunities to engage with numerous dedicated, conscientious educators who make every effort to differentiate instruction. We designed this chapter to reflect their questions and our responses.

Issue #1: *Yeah, I buy into what you are saying about the need for differentiated instruction, but it seems like I need to spend most of my time with small groups and individuals and I wonder what I am suppose to do with the rest of the students?*

We agree that differentiating instruction is more effectively done in grouping arrangements that allow you to work more closely with individuals or smaller similar achievement groups of students. But doing so without interruptions from the students who are not in the group leads to a major concern namely, what to do with the rest of the kids when working with an individual or a small group? This concern is so important that we addressed it in our previous work in which we present a chapter and an article on organizing and managing work away from the teacher (Opitz and Ford 2000, 2004/2005).

That being said, the question is so important that we actually designed the models we showcase in Chapters 3 through 6 to inherently address it. With Model 1: Grouping Without Tracking (Chapter 3), students are working together on the front and back end of the lesson. The students are primarily grouped for the actual reading and response to the text. While one group is working more directly with the teacher, receiving the additional support that they need to read and respond to the common core text, the other students are completing the same activity indirectly guided by the structure provided only with less direct face-to-face support. While some students may finish their work before the teacher completes work with the other group, a few additional tasks could be offered. For example, students who have completed their reading and responding can share with other students who have also completed all assigned tasks. If they are working with a common text like *Nory Ryan's Song*, students might be invited to explore other resources on immigration or books by Patricia Reilly Giff.

In Model 2: Jigsawing (Chapter 4), students are again working together on the front and back end of the lesson. During the reading and response to the text, all students are assigned to small groups. Each group is reading different parts of the text, but all are either guided directly by the teacher or indirectly guided by the structure provided. If multiple groups need additional support, the teacher can join those groups and provide direct assistance. Rove among the groups joining groups to provide differentiated support. There is still the possibility that one jigsaw group may finish before the others and they can scan the rest of the text they were not assigned while they are waiting. They can also explore additional resources related to the topic. Jigsawing provides a vehicle for rebuilding the community when all groups have completed their work. Students can be organized to report out to discuss across texts.

In Model 3: Connected Literature Circles (Chapter 5), the focus lesson is taught in a large group. Again, since all students are assigned to one of the literature circles, all should be engaged while the teacher provides more direct support to those groups that need more help. If the group should finish ahead of the other students, students can continue to read texts. In the primary lesson we described, for instance, the students could review the other ABC books used in the group. With the frontier theme we described for intermediate grades, they could keep moving forward in their chapter books or explore any of the other chapter books or related resources on frontier life. When all groups have completed their reading and responding, then all students can be brought back together and organized to discuss across texts.

Finally in Model 4: Focused Readers' Workshop (Chapter 6), the dilemma of what to do with the rest of the kids is addressed by keeping the students together for the focus lesson and bringing the group back together to work in responding collectively across texts they read individually. While reading, all students are engaged in the task the teacher structured so that you can differentiate levels of support when conferencing with individuals or small groups with similar needs. If students finish the task early, they can continue reading in their text. If they finish reading their text, they can select another one suitable for the focus of the workshop.

Besides designing the models so that they are considerate of the issue of what to do with the rest of the class, we offer four additional options to design work away from the teacher that will keep students independently engaged while the teacher differentiates instruction for individuals or small groups (Ford 2005a; Ford and Opitz 2002). Other options can be added to our list.

Option 1: Use parallel processes that allow for meaningful small-group and individual work away from the teacher. In one school district, the decision to move toward the use of differentiated instruction was somewhat complicated by the perceived need to create and manage a classroom infrastructure of centers and learning stations to keep learners engaged when they were working away from the teacher. At the same time, the district staff had made a long-term commitment to introducing writers' workshop with which many teachers had become very comfortable. Therefore, instead of working on implementing differentiated instruction and learning centers at the same time, the district literacy coaches encouraged teachers to see how they could use the structure of writers' workshop to engage students when not working on reading instruction with the teacher. Since writers' workshop provided times for learners to be engaged independently in planning, writing, revising, editing, and publishing their writing, it became what students did when they were not working with the teacher. In addition, writers' workshop provided meaningful opportunities for small peer groups to come together and help and share with one another. This small-group work provided another thing for students to do while the teacher worked with others in the class.

Option 2: Develop classroom structures that provide ongoing independent work that flows from classroom instruction for learners. In one first-grade classroom, common core poems were used as shared reading experiences. About once a month, the teacher introduced a new poem to the learners. The poem became a friendly and familiar vehicle for both oral language and reading fluency as well as word study in the large-group setting. But before retiring the poem, it became the basis for a series of activities for learners to complete independently. It worked well for this teacher because he had established a classroom structure and taught it to students before expecting them to complete it on their own. Children were taught how to be independent. Each learner had an independent poetry folder. In the folder, the learner had a hardcopy of the poem to use for repeated reading, which enabled meaningful fluency practice. The learner also created a set of cards based on the words contained in the poem and used them to complete matching activities. Finally, the teacher designed a reading/writing project for each poem. In all, then, for each poem introduced, the learners had at least four meaningful literacy activities they could accomplish away from the teacher. As the learners mastered one set of activities for one poem, new activities filled their folders as new poems were introduced. In this way, the folder always contained something that would keep learners meaningfully engaged away from the teacher. What's more is that the activities provided the teacher with yet another way to differentiate instruction. The activities were deliberately varied to address reader differences.

Option 3: Develop classroom structures that allow for small-group and independent inquiry projects as an ongoing alternative for engaging learners away from the teacher. Taking a cue from the work of gifted and talented educator Susan Winebrenner (2000), one district staff saw the need to have broader conversations about how to challenge learners when the learners had accomplished the expectations of the classroom curriculum. They decided to develop a districtwide infrastructure for small-group and independent inquiry projects. Doing so provided an ongoing meaningful activity for learners to engage in away from the teacher. The district's literacy coaches provided support and materials for teachers so that they could meet with success when introducing guidelines and explaining the planning sheets, contracts, and evaluation forms to their students. Since the process and procedures were consistent within grade levels and adjusted appropriately through the grades, learners grew familiar with them and built on them from year to year.

Option 4: Develop centers that allow for meaningful engagement of multiple individuals with a variety of print-related activities away from the teacher. Certainly centers are one common way to address the question of what to do with the rest of the students. But there is much to consider when designing and implementing centers as we have previously written (Ford and Opitz 2002). Those suggestions still hold true. In summary, we suggest the following:

- Build on classroom routines to encourage independent use by students and efficient use of teacher preparation time.

- Use centers where the structure can stay the same, but the activities within them can change with relative ease.

- Make centers accessible for all students while at the same time providing for individual differences by varying the level of sophistication each task demands of the learner.

- Link to what you know about students as readers, writers, and learners as well as to standards, curricula, and assessments.

- Keep simple structures so transition time can be kept to a minimum, equitable use can be encouraged, and accountability can be built in.

Issue #2 *Yeah, I can see how to provide differentiated instruction more directly to one similar achievement small group, but while I am doing that my other students never seem to work well in their groups. How do I get them to work better in small groups on their own?*

We agree that directly supporting students face-to-face in a small group is easier if you can be assured that your other students can be just as *productively* engaged more independently in other groups. But assuming that will happen without intentionally planning for it may lead to disappointing attempts to differentiate instruction.

So how does one prepare all students to participate effectively in independent small groups? We believe that much of the instruction begins with the way student interaction is structured, modeled, and encouraged in large-group activities. We need to actively show students how to include the voices of all students. Clearly if the goal is to keep all learners engaged during classroom activities, then making sure all voices are heard and honored is a critical first step. When learners realize that their voices are being ignored or marginalized, they are likely to disengage from active participation in the large group. Sometimes disengagement is voluntary—such as when students learn if they don't raise their hands and just remain quiet they can remove themselves from having to participate in large-group activities—sometimes it is not. Instead, group dynamics intentionally and unintentionally cause some students to silence their voices. Having techniques to systematically make sure that all voices are not only heard but honored in large groups is important for two reasons. First, the techniques will ensure a greater likelihood that learners will stay engaged during the whole-class activities. Second, these interaction techniques lay a foundation for small-group participation that honors all voices in the group.

But how do you get all students to participate in large groups—both in sharing their voices and listening to the voices of others? How do you encourage all students to participate effectively in small groups? We offer the following list of tried-and-true techniques for improving classroom participation. Some ideas work best for large groups. Others are better for small groups (Ford 2005b). We are convinced that adding techniques like these to your repertoire will help you to raise the level of engagement and guarantee that more voices are heard and honored.

Concrete Reminders. With some students—those with less experience and those who struggle in group settings—use concrete tools to remind everyone that all students should be allowed to have their voices heard in the group. One teacher of younger students we know brought in a chunk of carpet cut from a larger piece. He introduced the carpet as "the floor." He told students that whoever has the floor has the right to speak and when someone has the floor everyone else must listen. Once that person is done speaking, someone else can have the floor and have their turn to speak.

Random Assignments. Sometimes randomly assigning students roles can allow new voices to be heard in new group arrangements (though the randomness of the assignment can be a bit strategic if you carefully plan it ahead of time!). Teachers we know often use counting off to randomly assign students to teams and groups. Consider spelling out a word instead. For example, one teacher asks the students spell out the word *roles* one letter at a time. Teams of five are formed by making sure each group has one student with each of the letters in the word *roles*. The letters are then used to assign roles within the group: All *r*'s will be recorders, all *l*'s will be leaders, and all *s*'s will be spokespersons. Again this allows a random assignment of whose voices will be heard.

Formats. Sometimes we may be called on to work with students who have very little experience working effectively with others in groups. These students are limited in their ability to use language as a way of preparing to read, monitoring their reading, and responding to what was read in groups away from the teacher. For these students, especially, offer strong external support by creating structures that actually guide the group interaction even when the teacher is not with the group. These structures vary in their degree of explicitness but all provide direction to groups that seem less than able to direct themselves. The teacher could write short scripts that provide students with the language they need to guide the groups. For example, the leader of the group might be provided language that would be used in guiding the group through the pre-reading strategies for handling a piece of informational text. The script would help the students lead other members of their group through their brainstorming, predicting, and purpose setting. Another member of the group might be taught and scripted to help the group with monitoring their comprehension as they read through the text. A third member of the group would be taught and scripted to guide the group as it responds to the text. Again these scripts are often embedded with strategic language so that students learn the strategies as well as how to help each other in group activities.

Classroom Chemistry. Sometimes you simply need to mix up the response patterns in the classroom especially if they become static and predictable. When group formation and partner selection always leads to the same combinations, classroom interaction becomes a bit stale. The same students work with the same students and the same students report out and have their voices heard. Instead, consider using a variety of techniques to mix up the chemistry to deliberately shake up the interaction patterns and voices being heard in a classroom. Clock buddies is but one example. It works best for assigning partners. Every student in the class has a clock with one signature line at each hour. Students then take turns signing up on each other's clocks. You put your name at 12:00 on my clock and I put my name at 12:00 on your clock. By the time the signing is done, each student has twelve buddies, one assigned to each hour on the clock. Whenever the teacher wants students to work as partners, the teacher indicates what partner to work with, for example, "Today work with your three o'clock partners." Everyone checks out their clocks and finds their 3:00 buddy and begins to work. These kid of partnering techniques can be simplified for younger students (maybe you only have four buddies on your clock at 12, 3, 6 and 9 o'clock) or modified for longer periods of time (maybe you sign up on weekly calendars and have a partner for the day).

Monitoring. You may want to ask an outside observer to track interaction patterns in your classroom. Results are often surprising because despite intentional ongoing efforts to engage all students, some students are often overlooked in large- and small-group activities. Sometimes when we rely solely on our hearts and heads to keep track of what is happening, kids slip through the cracks. Some simple techniques for monitoring interaction in more concrete forms may help you to better keep track of what is really happening. For example, the class list on a clipboard may be the most useful tracking tool any teacher can have. Even with a very simple coding system, like putting a plus sign (+) for an appropriate response and a minus sign (–) for an inappropriate response next to a student's name after responding, the teacher or an outside observer (e.g., literacy coach) can track a large-group interaction pattern. The list of names provides a systematic way to call on students so that all voices are heard. Simple coding begins to reveal levels of engagement and understanding in large groups that can be use to document growth and learning and support evaluation decisions.

Group Processing. By building in systematic review of small-group work through self-evaluation, the teacher can strengthen students' social skills over time. These techniques will remind all students of what good group work looks, sounds, and feels like. There are numerous self-evaluation forms in commercial resources that can be easily adopted or adapted for this purpose. For instance, one social processing technique for groups is "We Like, We'll Try." Students in the group divide a paper in half. On one side students write "We Like" and on the other side they write "We'll Try." Collectively they list two to four things they liked abut how the group worked this time. Then they collectively decide on two to four ways they will try to improve the next time they meet. A brisk walk around the room by the teacher at the end of the lesson enables each group to share one or two "we like"s and "we'll try"s when prompted by the teacher to do so.

Without a doubt, to get the most out of these techniques designed to help students develop interpersonal skills so they can work together in small and large groups, the teacher will need to explicitly teach the following:

- Turn-taking strategies

- Listening strategies

- Ways to work with partners (looks like, sounds like)

- Ways to respond to each other (open-ended discussion starters)

- Ways to disagree with each other

- Ways to challenge each other

- Making good choices in groups

Effective interaction in large and small groups does not just happen. Like most skills, students need to be taught *how* to participate appropriately in these settings. Sometimes the use of practical techniques actually gives students a better sense of what it means when we say that all voices have the right to be heard and honored in the classroom community. Over time, we want students to internalize these inclusion ideas so that they can use them independently without our structures and interventions.

Issue #3 *Yeah, I would try to provide differentiated instruction to more individuals, but what if I have one of those classes where my students just can't work independently while I work with others?*

As we stated with small-group work, we cannot assume that just because we set up opportunities for students to work independently that they will be able to work *effectively* independently. We need to explicitly teach procedural and behavioral skills integrating minilessons that include this type of instruction. Here are our suggestions for fostering independent work skills in your students.

Gradually introduce independent work structures to students. Independent work structures should be modeled in the large group and practiced in small groups before expecting students to work independently. A potential flow might be as follows:

- Watch the teacher.

- Help the teacher.

- Student does in a group.

- Student does with a partner.

- Student does alone.

Introduce and open up independent work structures one at a time and gradually add more so students won't get overwhelmed or overstimulated by the tasks and choices. Introduce and review independent work structures to smaller groups of students to ensure that all have understood. The structures should help students see their ability to be able to work independently learning organization skills and how to take responsibility for their own learning.

Also keep in mind that the proportion of time devoted to independent work should be gradually increased from grade level to grade level and throughout the school year. Initially, work with the whole class so you can learn about your students before you adopt, modify, or create the structures for independent work.

Hold learners accountable! Accountability measures should be built into the independent structures to foster engagement and provide assessment information. Techniques for daily, weekly, monthly, and yearly assessment can be integrated easily. These might include:

- paper trails

- performances

- self-evaluations

- contracts

- learning centers records

- choice menus

- reading tickets

- center folders

- center boxes

Be sure to build in reminders for students to review and revisit independent work rules and routines. After independent work periods, build in time during the instructional block for processing collectively how well they worked during these times.

Issue #4 *Yeah, I can see the value of the four models, but how do I put them together to form a more comprehensive reading program?*

We are not recommending the exclusive use of any one of these models. To do so would magnify the flaws of that model and end up privileging some students, but not meeting the needs of all. We expect that you would weave in and out of the models and try to put them together in such a way that you create a more comprehensive reading program. Perhaps what you might think about is a three-phase approach. Thinking this way may also help you align the use of these models with the three tiers of Response to Intervention plans as well.

Phase One: Whole-Group Instruction. The most effective and efficient use of time and materials in classroom instruction is during whole-group instruction. Whole-group instruction allows the teacher to reach as many students as possible. The first goal of any classroom teachers is to provide the highest-quality whole-group instruction. If a teacher is reaching as many students as possible during whole-group instruction, the need to differentiate beyond that diminishes. In the models we presented, we emphasize a gradual release of responsibility. Each model begins with whole-group instruction in order to frontload the lessons with teacher modeling and demonstrating and guided practice with students in the large group. Each model also ends by rebuilding the classroom community bringing everyone back together to collectively respond to or make sense of the text. In addition, Model 1: Grouping Without Tracking provides one way to effectively enhance the quality of whole-group instruction. It might also be a good first step for teachers who are used to whole-group models for instruction and are looking to integrate more differentiation. For teachers beginning this change, the grouping without tracking model may be easier to start with because it holds the text and the task constant and asks teachers to first try to differentiate only their level of support.

Phase Two: Small-Group Instruction. Even when whole-group instruction is of the highest quality, it is not always possible to provide all students with what they need in a large-group setting. The second most effective and efficient use of time and materials in classroom instruction occurs during small-group instruction. The next goal is to provide an effective layer of small-group instruction. All classrooms need a layer that provides a structure for working with students in small groups. It becomes easier to target instruction when the group of students sitting before a teacher is smaller in size and similar in their achievement levels. If a teacher effectively uses small-group instruction, the need to differentiate further may be minimized. Model 2: Jigsawing provides one way to add that layer of small-group work. It might be a good way for a teacher to make a transition from exclusive use of whole-group instruction to beginning the use of some small-group instruction. With jigsawing, the teacher can keep the task constant and can work with a single text, but start to move toward the use of similar achievement groups to differentiate instruction as students read and respond. Jigsawing also provides a means for experimenting with mixed achievement groups as students start to work together across the divided text. Once teachers get comfortable with jigsawing, they might begin to move toward Model 3: Connected Literature Circles. This will require adding the ability to secure multiple related texts, but experiences with jigsawing should help both the teacher and the students be more prepared for the small-group work. Eventually, teachers might grow in their confidence and comfort and move small-group instruction toward greater variety in the tasks, texts, and support given to each small group targeting instruction even further.

Phase Three: Individualized Instruction. While it is not the most efficient or effective use of time and materials, all classrooms also need a layer of individualized instruction. Even with masterful whole-group instruction and effective differentiation during small groups, there are always a couple of students who need help with a couple of things for a couple more minutes. Our final goal is to provide a structure for individualized instruction. In one district, this was called *differentiated intervention.* All classrooms need a layer that provides a structure for working with students individually. It is the ultimate way to target instruction since even a small group of students can differ in their needs. Model 4: Focused Readers' Workshop is one way to provide for the need to work with individual students. Teachers who are increasingly comfortable with the other phases may find it easier to take this next step. Once teachers have used a focused workshop format for awhile, they may be more willing to open it up a bit more allowing for even further individualization.

We believe that if teachers can effectively weave together these three phases into their literacy program, the need for *intensive intervention* will be reduced significantly. Intensive intervention usually is the least efficient use of time since the student often has to leave the classroom literacy program to work with another professional. It's also not the most efficient use of resources since it often involves the significant cost of additional staff. As you can see, our thoughts are perfectly aligned with the spirit of Response to Intervention, reducing the number of referrals to special programs.

Figure 7–1 shows how a district staff might lay out their Response to Intervention plan for reading instruction. Notice the parallels in the three phases described above.

Issue #5 *Yeah, I want to try differentiation, but how will I know if I am doing it effectively?*

With so many different views of differentiation, it is no small wonder that this issue surfaces. And while there are several helpful references in Appendix A, the answer to this question is somewhat relative to the differentiation view to which each teacher subscribes.

Because we propose the grouping models as a convenient and practical way to differentiate instruction in a manageable way, and because each of these models uses a lesson structure that contains the same three elements (frontloading, reading and responding, and extending), we propose that you use the reflection form shown in Figure 7–2.

Figure 7–1 *Sample Response to Intervention Plan for Reading Instruction*

Tier Name	Overall Goal	Features and How They Work
Tier I—Universal Options	To enhance success and reduce barriers to learning for a majority of students.	• All students in classroom receive like instruction • Instruction is implemented by classroom teacher • Takes place in regular classroom setting • Some differentiation is provided to help students with common curriculum • Assessment informs whether further instruction is needed
Tier II—Selected Options	To provide supplemental options to small groups of students who have yet to meet benchmarks.	• Is meant for those students who are among the lowest ten to fifteen performers in their grade-level group • *Exists congruently with* regular classroom instruction • Can be implemented by either classroom teacher or specialized staff: reading specialist, literacy coordinator, or ELL, for example • Can be provided in or out of the regular classroom setting • Teacher provides targeted instruction, which can focus on phonemic awareness, phonics, vocabulary, comprehension, and fluency • Any writing instruction focuses only as it relates to reading
Tier III—Targeted Options	To provide intensive instruction as needed per student performance in Tier II.	• Intended for students with a high likelihood of developing a lasting pattern of reading failure • Needed by very few students • Instruction is specifically designed and customized to address individual children's identified needs • Can be implemented by classroom teacher or specialized staff • Progress is monitored frequently • Teacher provides more intense instruction, which can focus on phonemic awareness, phonics, vocabulary, comprehension, and fluency; writing instruction focuses on its relationship to reading

Figure 7–2 *Key Questions to Consider When Reflecting on Your Efforts to Foster Differentiation and Engagement*

Reading Lesson: _____ Date: _____

Lesson Component	Question	Thoughts/Ideas
Frontloading	1. Did I provide all students with new information and avoid assuming that all students would come to the lesson with the same background knowledge? 2. Did I intentionally involve all students in the frontloading activities, deliberately inviting students who may become less engaged into the discussions or other activities?	
Reading and Responding	1. Did I gradually release responsibility for reading and responding to students withdrawing support as appropriate? 2. Did I identify meaningful tasks for students to complete if they finish early and am I still providing support for students in need?	
Extending	1. Did I use graphic tools that produce a visual summary of what was learned and create a paper trail that I can use to informally assess students? 2. Did I review what was learned during the lesson with all students?	
Overall	1. Did I provide for individual differences by differentiating my levels of support throughout the lesson? 2. Did I provide for individual differences by differentiating text selections assigned to groups or individuals?	

Issue #6 *Yeah, I can see the value of using the four models as a practical way to differentiate instruction, but as a literacy coach or reading specialist, how can I best help others to best understand differentiation and how to use the models to better ensure practical differentiation?*

We can only begin with ourselves. If we *show* as much or even more so than *tell*, others are better able to see themselves doing exactly what we are doing and therefore see it as manageable and doable. We offer the following suggestions.

- Brainstorm with participants ways that they currently feel they differentiate instruction. Make some sort of visual display of these ideas and revisit them after all have had some time to examine the models. Used this way, you can use their brainstormed list as a pre- and post-assessment of their understandings.

- You will notice that every lesson in Chapters 3 through 6 is sprinkled with annotations that show how the various teachers are differentiating instruction. These annotations can serve as a launch into having participants examine the lessons for additional ways that differentiation is occurring that are not mentioned in the annotations.

- Have participants examine the first four issues previously explained for ways to differentiate instruction. Have small groups make a list of these differentiation ideas that are embedded into the suggestions.

- Demonstrate all four of the grouping models. Using several of the references we show in Appendix A, take the learners through the models one at a time on four different occasions depending on how much time you have for any one session. Consider the following process we often use when we present on this topic:

  - Make a copy of the lesson plan form for the model you want to demonstrate. (See Appendix B for all necessary forms.)

  - Choose the reading material you will use with the participants.

  - Write out your plan including all three phases of the lesson as shown on the form.

  - Make a transparency of your lesson plan.

  - Make a copy of the blank lesson plan form for participants.

  - Gather your resources.

- Teach the lesson.

- Using the transparency that shows your lesson, make explicit for participants what they just did as they write pertinent information on their blank lesson plan forms.

- Discuss ways that differentiation occurred during the demonstration.

- Close the staff development session by having each participant reflect on the ways that you demonstrated differentiation throughout the entire staff development session. One question we often use to get this reflection going is, "So how did I differentiate my instruction today?" As yet another way to drive home just how much you use differentiation, you might want to write their ideas on a whiteboard, chart, or transparency so that all have a visual reminder of what you did. You could also have them write one idea on a sticky note, pair-share with a partner, and then report out to the large group.

Bibliography of Professional Resources

Differentiation

Adams, Cheryll, and Rebecca Pierce. 2006. *Differentiating Instruction: A Practical Guide to Tiered Lessons in the Elementary Grades*. Waco, TX: Prufrock.

Armstrong, Thomas. 1998. *Awakening Genius in the Classroom*. Alexandria, VA: Association for Supervision and Curriculum Development.

Bender, William, and Carla Shores. 2007. *Response to Intervention: A Practical Guide for Every Teacher*. Thousand Oaks, CA: Corwin.

Coil, Carolyn, and Rita King. 2007. *Successful Teaching in the Differentiated Classroom*. Marion, IL: Pieces of Learning.

Dodge, Judith. 2006. *Differentiation in Action: A Complete Resource with Research-Supported Strategies to Help You Plan and Organize Differentiated Instruction and Achieve Success with All Learners*. New York: Scholastic.

Drapwau, Patti. 2004. *Differentiated Instruction: Making It Work*. New York: Scholastic.

Ford, Michael. 2005. *Differentiation Through Flexible Grouping: Successfully Reaching All Readers*. Naperville, IL: Learning Point Associates.

Forsten, Char, Gretchen Goodman, Jim Grant, Betty Hollas, and Donna Whyte. 2006. *The More Ways You TEACH, the More Students You REACH: 86 Strategies for Differentiating Instruction*. Peterborough, NH: Crystal Springs.

Forsten, Char, Jim Grant, and Betty Hollas. 2001. *Differentiated Instruction: Different Strategies for Different Learners*. Peterborough, NH: Crystal Springs.

———. 2003. *Differentiating Textbooks: Strategies to Improve Student Comprehension and Motivation*. Peterborough, NH: Crystal Springs.

Gregory, Gayle, and Carolyn Chapman. 2007. *Differentiated Instructional Strategies: One Size Doesn't Fit All*. 2d ed. Thousand Oaks, CA: Corwin.

Gregory, Gayle, and Lin Kuzmich. 2004. *Differentiated Literacy Strategies for Student Growth and Achievement in Grades K–6*. Thousand Oaks, CA: Corwin.

Heacox, Diane. 2002. *Differentiating Instruction in the Classroom: How to Reach and Teach All Learners, Grades 3–12*. Minneapolis, MN: Free Spirit.

Hollas, Betty. 2005. *Differentiating Instruction in a Whole-Group Setting: Taking the Easy First Steps into Differentiation.* Peterborough, NH: Crystal Springs.

Marzano, Robert, Debra Pickering, and Jane Pollock. 2001. *Classroom Instruction That Works: Research-Based Strategies for Increasing Student Achievement.* Alexandria, VA: Association for Supervision and Curriculum Development.

Moll, Anne, ed. 2003. *Differentiated Instruction Guide for Inclusive Teaching Grades 3–12.* Port Chester, NY: Dude.

Owocki, Gretchen. 2005. *Time for Literacy Centers: How to Organize and Differentiate Instruction.* Portsmouth, NH: Heinemann.

Pavelka, Pat. 2005. *Differentiated Assignments.* Peterborough, NH: Crystal Springs.

Robb, Laura. 2008. *Differentiating Reading Instruction: How to Teach Reading to Meet the Needs of Each Student.* New York: Scholastic.

Silver, Debbie. 2003. *Drumming to the Beat of a Different Marcher: Finding the Rhythm for Teaching a Differentiated Classroom.* Nashville, TN: Incentive.

Sprenger, Marilee. 2003. *Differentiation Through Learning Styles and Memory.* Thousand Oaks, CA: Corwin.

———. 2005. *How to Teach So Students Remember.* Alexandria, VA: Association for Supervision and Curriculum Development.

Smitny, Joan Franklin, and S. E. Von Fremd. 2004. *Differentiating for the Young Child: Teaching Strategies Across the Content Areas (K–3).* Thousand Oaks, CA: Corwin Press.

Thousand, Jacqueline, Richard Villa, and Ann Novin. 2007. *Differentiating Instruction: Collaborative Planning and Teaching for Universally Designed Learning.* Thousand Oaks, CA: Corwin Press.

Tilton, Linda. 2003. *The Teacher's Toolbox for Differentiating Instruction: 700 Strategies, Tips, Tools and Techniques.* Shorewood, MN: Covington Cove.

Tomlinson, Carol. 2003. *Fulfilling the Promise of the Differentiated Classroom: Strategies and Tools for Responsive Teaching.* Alexandria, VA: Association for Supervision and Curriculum Development.

Tomlinson, Carol, and Caroline Eidson. 2003. *Differentiation in Practice: A Resource Guide for Differentiating Curriculum, Grades K–5.* Alexandria, VA: Association for Supervision and Curriculum Development.

Tomlinson, Carol, and Jay McTighe. 2006. *Integrating Differentiated Instruction—Understanding by Design.* Alexandria, VA: Association for Supervision and Curriculum Development.

Yatvin, Joanne. 2004. *A Room with a Differentiated View: How to Serve ALL Children as Individual Learners.* Portsmouth, NH: Heinemann.

Differentiation Websites

www.help4teachers.com
www.Kidsourcew.com/kidsource/content/diff_instruction.html
www.piecesoflearning.com
www.ascd.org
www.caroltomlinson.com
www.Paulakluth.com
www.read/write.org

Flexible Grouping

Caldwell, Leslie, and Michael Ford. 2002. *Where Have All the Bluebirds Gone? How to Soar with Flexible Grouping*. Portsmouth, NH: Heinemann.

Cohen, Elizabeth. 1994. *Designing Groupwork: Strategies for the Heterogeneous Classroom*. 2d ed. New York: Teachers College.

Daley, Allyson. 2007. *Partner Reading: A Way to Help All Readers Grow*. New York: Scholastic.

Diller, Debbie. 2007. *Making the Most of Small Groups: Differentiation for All*. Portland, ME: Stenhouse.

Nagel, Greta. 2001. *Effective Grouping for Literacy Instruction*. New York: Allyn & Bacon.

Opitz, Michael. 1998. *Flexible Grouping in Reading: Practical Ways to Help All Students Become Better Readers*. New York: Scholastic.

Opitz, Michael, and Michael Ford. 2001. *Reaching Readers: Flexible and Innovative Strategies for Guided Reading*. Portsmouth, NH: Heinemann.

Radencich, Margaret, and L. McKay. 1995. *Flexible Grouping for Literacy in the Elementary Grades*. Needham Heights, MA: Allyn & Bacon.

Tyner, Beverly. 2004. *Small Group Reading Instruction: A Differentiated Teaching Model for Beginning and Struggling Readers*. Newark, DE: International Reading Association.

Tyner, Beverly, and Sharon Green. 2005. *Small Group Reading Instruction: A Differentiated Teaching Model for Intermediate Readers, Grades 3–8*. Newark, DE: International Reading Association.

Wrubel, Ronit. 2002. *Great Grouping Strategies: Dozens of Ways to Flexibly Group Your Students for Maximum Learning Across the Curriculum*. New York: Scholastic.

Independent Learning/Organization

Cunningham, Patricia, and Richard Allington. 1994. *Classrooms That Work: They Can All Read and Write*. 4th ed. New York: HarperCollins.

Daniels, Harvey, and Nancy Steinke. 2004. *Mini-lessons for Literature Circles*. Portsmouth, NH: Heinemann.

Diffily, Deborah, and Charlotte Sassman. 2006. *Managing Independent Reading: Effective Classroom Routines*. New York: Scholastic.

Finney, Susan. 2000. *Keep the Rest of the Class Reading & Writing While You Teach Small Groups*. New York: Scholastic.

Goldberg, Gravity, and Jennifer Serravallo. 2007. *Conferring with Readers: Supporting Each Student's Growth and Independence*. Portsmouth, NH: Heinemann.

Pavelka, Patricia. 1999. *Create Independent Learners: Teacher-Tested Strategies for ALL Ability Levels*. Peterborough, NH: Crystal Springs.

Serafini, Frank, and Suzette Youngs. 2006. *Around the Reading Workshop in 180 Days: A Month-by-Month Gguide to Effective Instruction*. Portsmouth, NH: Heinemann.

Witherall, Nancy. 2007. *The Guided Reading Classroom: How to Keep ALL Students Working Constructively*. Portsmouth, NH: Heinemann.

Inquiry Approaches

Chard, Sylvia. 1998. *The Project Approach: Book One—Making Curriculum Come Alive*. New York: Scholastic.

———. 1998. *The Project Approach: Book Two—Managing Successful Projects*. New York: Scholastic.

Harvey, Stephanie. 1998. *Nonfiction Matters: Reading, Writing and Research in Grades 3–8*. Portland, ME: Stenhouse.

Helm, Judy, and Sallee Beneke, eds. 2003. *The Power of Projects: Meeting Contemporary Challenges in Early Childhood Classrooms, Strategies, and Solutions*. New York: Teachers College Press.

Helm, Judy, and Lillian Katz. 2001. *Young Investigators: The Project Approach in the Early Years*. New York: Teachers College Press.

Katz, Lillian, and Sylvia Chard. 2000. *Engaging Children's Minds: The Project Approach*. 2d ed. Stamford, CT: Ablex.

Learning Centers

Allen, Irene, and Susan Perry. 2000. *Literacy Centers: What Your Other Kids Do During Guided Reading Groups*. Huntington Beach, CA: Creative Teaching Press.

Diller, Debbie. 2005. *Practice with Purpose: Literacy Work Stations for Grades 3–6*. Portland, ME: Stenhouse.

Holliman, Linda. 2001. *Center Set Up: Fun Ideas for Setting Up 16 Literacy Workstations*. Huntington Beach, CA: Creative Teaching Press.

Ingraham, Phoebe Bell. 1997. *Creating and Managing Learning Centers: A Thematic Approach*. Peterborough, NH: Crystal Springs.

Nations, Susan, and Mellissa Alonso. 2001. *Primary Literacy Centers: Making Reading and Writing STICK*. Gainesville, FL: Maupin House.

Opitz, Michael. 1994. *Learning Centers: Getting Them Started, Keeping Them Going*. New York: Scholastic.

Teaching English Language Learners

Akhavan, Nancy. 2006. *Help! My Kids Don't All Speak English: How to Set Up a Language Workshop in Your Linguistically Diverse Classroom*. Portsmouth, NH: Heinemann.

Bouchard, Margaret. 2005. *Comprehension Strategies for English Language Learners*. New York: Scholastic.

Boyd-Batstone, Paul. 2006. *Differentiated Early Literacy for English Language Learners: Practical Strategies*. New York: Allyn & Bacon.

Brock, Cynthia H., and Taffy E. Raphael. 2005. *Windows to Language, Literacy, and Culture: Insights from an English Language Learner*. Newark, DE: International Reading Association.

Buhrow, Brad, and Anne Upczak Garcia. 2006. *Ladybugs, Tornadoes, and Swirling Galaxies: English Language Learners Discover Their World Through Inquiry*. Portland, ME: Stenhouse.

Cappellini, Mary. 2005. *Balancing Reading and Language Learning: A Resource for Teaching English Language Learners, K–5*. Portland, ME: Stenhouse and Newark, DE: International Reading Association.

Diaz-Rico, Lynne T. 2004. *Teaching English Learners: Strategies and Methods*. Boston: Allyn & Bacon.

Farrell, Thomas. 2006. *Succeeding with English Language Learners: A Guide for Beginning Teachers*. Thousand Oaks, CA: Corwin Press.

Freeman, Yvonne S., and David E. Freeman. 2006. *Teaching Reading and Writing in Spanish and English in Bilingual and Dual Language Classrooms*, 2d ed. Portsmouth, NH: Heinemann.

Houk, Farin. 2005. *Supporting English Language Learners: A Guide for Teachers and Administrators*. Portsmouth, NH: Heinemann.

IRA Study Group English Learners Module Collection. 2004. Newark, DE: International Reading Association.

Parker, Emelie, and Tess Pardini. 2006. *"The Words Came Down!" English Language Learners Read, Write, and Talk Across the Curriculum*. Portland, ME: Stenhouse.

Samway, Katherine Davies. 2006. *When English Language Learners Write: Connecting Research to Practice, K–8*. Portsmouth, NH: Heinemann.

Young, Terrell A., and Nancy L. Hadaway. 2006. *Supporting the Literacy Development of English Learners Increasing Success in All Classrooms*. Newark, DE: International Reading Association.

Teaching Special Learners

Bender, William. 2002. *Differentiating Instruction for Students with Learning Disabilities: Best Teaching Practices for General and Special Educators*. Thousand Oaks, CA: Corwin Press.

Burke, Kay. 2001. *What to Do with the Kid Who . . . : Developing Cooperation, Self-Discipline, and Responsibility in the Classroom*. Upper Saddle River, NY: Pearson.

McGrath, Constance. 2007. *The Inclusion-Classroom Problem-Solver: Structures and Supports to Serve All Learners*. Portsmouth, NH: Heinemann.

Renzulli, Joseph. 2001. *Enriching Curriculum for All Students*. Minneapolis, MN: Skylight.

Scala, Marilyn. 2001. *Working Together: Reading and Writing in Inclusive Classrooms*. Newark, DE: International Reading Association.

Smutny, Joan, Sally Walker, Elizabeth Meckstroth. 1997. *Teaching Young Gifted Kids in the Regular Classroom: Identifying, Nurturing and Challenging Ages 4–9*. Minneapolis, MN: Free Spirit.

Winebrenner, Susan, and Pamela Espeland. 1996. *Teaching Kids with Learning Difficulties in the Regular Classroom: Strategies and Techniques Every Teacher Can Use to Challenge and Motivate Struggling Students*. Minneapolis, MN: Free Spirit.

Blank Lesson Plan Forms

Grouping Without Tracking Lesson Plan

Content Area: _____

Content Objective: _____

Comprehension Objective: _____

Text(s)	
Frontloading (Before Reading) • Whole Class	
Reading and Responding (During Reading) • Groups	
Extending (After Reading)	

© 2008 by Michael F. Opitz and Michael P. Ford, from *Do-able Differentiation: Varying Groups, Texts, and Supports to Reach Readers*. Portsmouth, NH: Heinemann.

Jigsaw Lesson Plan

Content Area: _____

Content Objective: _____

Comprehension Objective: _____

Text(s)	
Frontloading (Before Reading) • **Whole Class**	
Reading and Responding (During Reading) • **Groups**	
Extending (After Reading)	

Connected Literature Circles Lesson Plan

Content Area: _____

Content Objective: _____

Comprehension Objective: _____

Texts	1.	
	2.	
	3.	
	4.	
Frontloading (Before Reading) • Whole Class		
Reading and Responding (During Reading) • Groups		
Extending (After Reading)		

Focused Readers' Workshop Lesson Plan

Content Area: _____

Content Objective: _____

Comprehension Objective: _____

Texts	
Frontloading (Before Reading) • Whole Class	
Reading and Responding (During Reading) • Individuals	
Extending (After Reading) • Teams or Triads	

CHILDREN'S LITERATURE CITED

Aardema, V. 1981. (Reteller) *Bringing the Rain to Kapiti Plain*. New York: Scholastic.

Baker, L. 2003. *The Animal ABC*. New York: Holt.

Brink, C. 2007. *Caddie Woodlawn*. New York: Aladdin.

Chandra, D. 1999. *A Is for Amos*. New York: Farrar, Straus & Giroux.

Cutting, J. 1998. *The Merry-Go-Round*. Bothell, WA: Wright Group.

Falls, C. B. 1998. *ABC Book*. New York: Morrow.

Fleischman, P. 1993. *The Borning Room*. New York: HarperTrophy.

Grover, M. 1993. *The Accidental Zucchini: An Unexpected Alphabet*. San Diego: Harcourt.

Hanly, S. 1997. *The Big Book of Animals*. New York: DK.

Isadora, R. 1999. *ABC Pop!* New York: Penguin.

Lester, A. 1996. *Alice and Aldo*. Boston: Houghton Mifflin.

Leunn, N. 1998. *Celebration of Light*. New York: Atheneum.

MacLachlan, S. 2004. *Sarah Plain and Tall*. New York: Scholastic.

Reilly Giff, P. 2000. *Nory Ryan's Song*. New York: Scholastic.

Rylant, C. 2002. *When I Was Young in the Mountains*. New York: Dutton.

Sabuda, R. 1998. *ABC Disney: An Alphabet Pop-Up*. New York: Disney.

Stine, M. 1992. *The Story of Laura Ingalls Wilder, Pioneer Girl*. New York: Yearling.

Whelan, G. 2002. *The Wanigan: A Life on the River*. New York: Knopf.

Alllington, R. 2006. *What Really Matters for Struggling Readers: Designing Research-Based Programs*. 2d ed. New York: Allyn & Bacon.

Allington, R., and P. Cunningham. 1996. *Schools That Work*. New York: Harper-Collins.

Allington, R., and P. Johnson, eds. 2002. *Reading to Learn: Lessons from Exemplary Fourth-Grade Classrooms*. New York: Guilford.

Allington, R., and S. Walmsley, eds. 2007. *No Quick Fix: The RTI Edition*. Newark, DE: International Reading Association.

Atwell, N. 1987. *In the Middle*. Portsmouth, NH: Heinemann.

———. 2007. *The Reading Zone*. New York: Scholastic.

Baker, L., and A. Wigfield. 1999. "Dimensions of Children's Motivation for Reading and Their Relations to Reading Activity and Achievement." *Reading Research Quarterly* 34: 4552–77.

Betts, E. 1946. *Foundations of Reading Instruction*. New York: American Book Company.

Clay, M. 1991. *Becoming Literate: The Construction of Inner Control*. Portsmouth, NH: Heinemann.

Costa, A., and B. Kallick. 2000. *Habits of Mind: A Developmental Series*. Alexandria, VA: Association for Supervision and Curriculum Development.

Dunn, K., and R. Dunn. 1987. "Dispelling Outmoded Beliefs About Student Learning." *Educational Leadership* 44: 55–63.

Edmunds, K., and K. Bauserman. 2006. "What Teachers Can Learn About Reading Motivation Through Conversations with Children." *The Reading Teacher* 59: 414–24.

Fitzgerald, J. 1999. "What Is This Thing Called 'Balance'?" *The Reading Teacher* 53: 100–107.

Ford, M. 2005a. *Differentiation Through Flexible Grouping: Successfully Reaching All Readers*. Naperville, IL: Learning Point Associates.

———. 2005b. "Improving Classroom Participation by Engaging and Honoring ALL Voices in Groups." *Colorado Reading Council Journal* 16: 13–17.

Ford, M., and M. Opitz. 2002. "Using Centers to Engage Children During Guided Reading Time: Intensifying Learning Experiences Away from the Teacher." *The Reading Teacher* 55: 710–17.

Freeman, D. E., and Y. S. Freeman. 2007. *English Language Learners: The Essential Guide*. New York: Scholastic.

Gardner, H. 1983. *Frames of Mind: The Theory of Multiple Intelligences*. New York: Basic Books.

Goleman, D. 1995. *Emotional Intelligence*. New York: Bantam.

Gregoric, L. 1982. *Inside Styles: Beyond the Basics*. Columbia, CT: Gregoric Associates.

Guthrie, J., and A. Wigfield. 1997. *Reading Engagement: Motivating Readers Through Integrated Instruction*. Newark, DE: International Reading Association.

Jensen, E. 2007. *Introduction to Brain-Compatible Learning*. 2d ed. Thousand Oaks, CA: Corwin.

Kolb, D. 1984. *Experiential Learning: Experience as the Source of Learning and Development*. Englewood Cliffs, NJ: Prentice Hall.

Kucer, S. 2005. *Dimensions of Literacy: A Conceptual Base for Teaching Reading and Writing in School Settings*. 2d ed. Mahwah, NJ: Erlbaum.

McCarthy, B. 2006. *Teaching Around the 4MAT Cycle: Designing Instruction for Diverse Learners with Diverse Learning Styles*. Thousand Oaks, CA: Corwin.

McKeown, R., and J. Gentilucci. 2007. "Think-Aloud Strategy: Metacognitive Development and Monitoring Comprehension in the Middle School Second-Language Classroom." *Journal of Adolescent & Adult Literacy* 51: 136–47.

National Association of State Directors of Special Education (NASDE) and Council of Administrators of Special Education (CASE). 2006. "Response to Intervention: NASDSE and CASE White Paper of RTI." (Retrieved from www.nasdse.org.)

Opitz, M., and M. Ford. 2000. *Reaching Readers: Flexible and Innovative Strategies for Guided Reading*. Portsmouth, NH: Heinemann.

———. 2004/2005. "What Do I Do with the Rest of the Kids? Ideas for Meaningful Independent Activities During Small-Group Reading Instruction." *The Reading Teacher* 58: 394–96.

———. 2006. *Books and Beyond: New Ways to Reach Readers*. Portsmouth, NH: Heinemann.

Paratore, J. 1990. *Classroom Contexts for Literacy Training: Flexible Grouping*. Paper presented at the Wisconsin State Reading Association Fall Conference, 5–6 October, Eau Claire, WI.

P.L. 108–446. 2004. *The Individuals with Disabilities Education Improvement Act of 2004*. Washington, DC: U.S. Department of Education.

Pressley, M. 2005. *Reading Instruction That Works: The Case for Balanced Teaching*. New York: Guilford.

Reed, B., and J. Railsbeck. 2003. *Strategies and Resources for Mainstream Teachers of English Language Learners*. Portland, OR: Northwest Regional Laboratory.

Reutzel. D. R., and R. Cooter. 1991. "Organizing for Effective Instruction: The Reading Workshop." *The Reading Teacher* 44: 548–54.

———. 2008. *Teaching Children to Read: The Teacher Makes the Difference*. 5th ed. New York: Allyn & Bacon.

Schwartz, P., and P. Kluth. 2007. *You're Welcome: Differentiating Instruction in the Inclusive Classroom*. Portsmouth, NH: Heinemann.

Silver, H., R. Strong, and M. Perini. 2000. *So Each May Learn: Integrating Learning Styles and Multiple Intelligences*. Alexandria, VA: Association for Supervision and Curriculum Development.

Sternberg, R. 1996. *Successful Intelligence: How Practical and Creative Intelligence Determine Success in Life*. New York: Simon & Schuster.

Taylor, B., P. D. Pearson, K. Clark, and S. Walpole. 2000. "Effective Schools and Accomplished Teachers: Lessons About Primary Grade Reading Instruction in Low-Income Schools." *Elementary School Journal* 101: 121–66.

Tomlinson, C. 1999. *The Differentiated Classroom: Responding to the Needs of All Learners*. Alexandria, VA: Association for Supervision and Curriculum Development.

Valencia, S., and M. Buly. 2004. "Behind Test Scores: What Struggling Readers *Really* Need." *The Reading Teacher* 57: 520–31.

Walpole, S., and M. McKenna. 2007. *Differentiated Reading Instruction: Strategies for the Primary Grades*. New York: Guildford.

Wharton-McDonald, R., M. Pressley, and J. M. Hampston. 1998. "Literacy Instruction in Nine First-Grade Classrooms: Teacher Characteristics and Student Achievement." *The Elementary School Journal* 99: 101–28.

Winebrenner, S. 2000. *Teaching Gifted Kids in the Regular Classroom: Strategies and Techniques Every Teacher Can Use to Meet the Academic Needs of the Gifted and Talented*. Rev. ed. Minneapolis, MN: Free Spirit.

Wormeli, R. 2007. *Differentiation: From Planning to Practice Grades 6–12*. Portland, ME: Stenhouse.

INDEX

Aardema, Verna, *Bringing the Rain to Kapiti Plain*, 36–43

Ablow, Gail, *Horse in the House and Other Strange But True Animal Stories, A*, 68

accountable, holding learners, 121

achievement, similar and mixed, 28–29

activity differentiation during reading instruction, 5

Adler, David, *Heroes for Civil Rights*, 68

affective knowledge, 6, 9–14

affective styles, differentiation, 3

Allington, R., 1

Allington, R., and P. Cunningham, *Schools That Work*, 28–29

Allington, R., and P. Johnson, *Reading to Learn: Lessons from Exemplary Fourth-Grade Classrooms*, 21–22

Allington, R., and S. Walmsley, *No Quick Fix: The RTI Edition*, 15–16

alphabet, books about, 75–81, 88–89

animals, books about, 68, 109–110

Arnold, Caroline, *South American Animals*, 111

Arnosky, Jim, *Manatee Morning, A*, 110

Arnosky, Jim, *Turtles, All About*, 109

Ashman, Linda, *Castles, Caves, and Honeycombs*, 109

Atwell, Nancie, *In the Middle*, 94–95

Atwell, Nancie, *Reading Zone, The*, 95

Avi, *Bright Shadow*, 90

Baker, L., and A. Wigfield, "Dimensions of Children's Motivation for Reading and Their Relations to Reading Activity and Achievement," *Reading Research Quarterly*, 9, 12

Baker, Leslie, *Animal ABC, The*, 76–77

Bartoletti, Susan Campbell, *Coal Miner's Bride, A: The Diary of Anetka Kaminska*, 49

beliefs about differentiated instruction
    addressing contemporary classroom demands, 14–16
    addressing the needs of English Language Learners (ELL), 16–17
    needs to address four critical elements, 4–6
    targeting key outcomes of a balanced literacy program, 6–14
    teachers matter, 17–22

Berger, Gilda, and Melvin Berger, list of authors' books, 68

Betts, E., *Foundations of Reading Instruction*, 29–30

books, lists of children's
    alphabet, 76, 88–89
    animals, 68, 109–10
    color and shape, 89–90
    courage, 90
    famous women, 90–91
    friendship and humorous stories, 91
    for grouping without tracking, 48–50
    for jigsawing, 68
    list of literature cited, 140
    mystery and survival, 92
    westward expansion and pioneer life, 81–87

Bowen, Betsy, *Tracks in the Wild*, 111

Brink, Carol Ryrie, *Caddie Woodlawn*, 81–87

Bruchac, Joseph, *Eagle Song*, 90

Byars, Betsy, *Trouble River*, 92

categories that motivate children's reading chart, 13

Chandra, Deborah, *A Is for Amos*, 76–77

children's literature cited, list of, 140

circle groups, connected literature, 85

classroom chemistry, altering, 118

Clay, M., *Becoming Literate: The Construction of Inner Control*, 4

Collard, Sneed, III, *B Is for Big Sky Country: A Montana Alphabet*, 88

color, books about, 89

connected literature circles

general teaching suggestions, 71–74

intermediate grade lesson, illustration of, 81–87

lesson plan form, 138

overview, 26

primary lesson, illustration of, 75–81

scenario and explanation, 69–71

context differentiation during reading instruction, 5–6

Costa, A., and B. Kallick, *Habits of Mind: A Developmental Series*, 3

Council of Administrators of Special Education (CASE), 14

courage, books about, 90

Cowley, Joy, *Chameleon, Chameleon*, 110

Crowther, Robert, *Colors*, 89

Cutting, Jillian, *Merry-Go-Round, The*, 8

Davidson, Margaret, *Helen Keller*, 90

Davies, Nicola, *Surprising Sharks*, 111

DeClements, Barthe, *Nothing's Fair in Fifth Grade*, 91

developmental levels, differentiation, 3

differentiated instruction

our beliefs about, 4–22

what it is, 1–4

differentiated instruction, issues. *See* issues, in differentiating instruction

differentiation

and engagement, questions to consider, 125

list of resources, 129–30

orientation chart, 3

Dixon, Dougal, *Amazing Dinosaurs: More Feathers, More Claws, Big Horn, Wide Jaws!*, 68

Dodds, Dale, *Shape of Things, The*, 90

Doyle, Malachy, *Cow*, 110

Duncan, Pamela, *Wacky Wedding, The: A Book of Alphabet Antics*, 89

Dunn, K., and R. Dunn, "Dispelling Outmoded Beliefs About Student Learning," *Educational Leadership*, 3

Dunphy, Madeleine, *Here Is . . .* titles, 48–49

Dunphy, Madeleine, *Here Is the Wetland*, 110

Dyer, Alan, *Space*, 68

Earle, Sylvia, *Hello, Fish! Visiting the Coral Reef*, 110

Edmunds, K., and K. Bauserman, "What Teachers Can Learn About Reading Motivation Through Conversations with Children," *Reading Teacher, The*, 12–13

Education Improvement Act (IDEA), 2, 14

Ehlert, Lois, *Color Zoo*, 89

elements, key

connected literature circles, 72

focused readers' workshop, 96

grouping without tracking, 33

jigsawing, 54

ELLs, ways to differentiate chart, 20

English Language Learners (ELL), 16–17, 132–33

English language proficiency levels charts, 18–19

extending

connected literature circles, 74, 77, 80–81, 84, 86–87

explanation of, 25

grouping without tracking, 36, 39, 42–43, 45, 48

jigsawing, 56, 59, 62–63, 65, 67

questions to consider, 125

reminders, 29

workshop, focused readers', 99–100, 102–104, 106, 108–109

Falls, C. B., *ABC Book*, 76–77

Falwell, Cathryn, *Shape . . .* titles, 90

Ferris, Jeri, *Walking the Road to Freedom*, 91

Fisher, Valore, *Ellsworth's Extraordinary Electric Ears and Other Amazing Alphabet Anecdotes*, 88

Fitzgerald, J., "What Is This Thing Called 'Balance'?" *Reading Teacher, The*, 6

Fleischman, Paul, *Borning Room, The*, 104–109

flexible grouping, list of resources, 131

focused readers' workshop. *See* workshop, focused readers'

folktale class matrix, 40

Ford, M., and M. Opitz, "Using Centers to Engage Children During Guided Reading Time: Intensifying Learning Experiences Away from the Teacher," *Reading Teacher, The*, 114–15

Ford, M., *Differentiation Through Flexible Grouping: Successfully Reaching All Readers*, 117

formats, for working in groups, 117–18

forms, 135–39

Freedman, Russell, *Immigrant Kids*, 50

Freeman, D. E., and Y. S. Freeman, *English Language Learners: The Essential Guide*, 16

friendship, books about, 91

frontloading

connected literature circles, 73, 75–79, 82–85

explanation of, 25

grouping without tracking, 34–35, 38–41, 43–47

jigsawing, 55, 57–60, 63–64

frontloading (*continued*)
  questions to consider, 125
  reminders, 29
  workshop, focused readers', 98, 100–102, 104–107

Gag, Wanda, *ABC Bunny, The*, 88
Gardner, H., *Frames of Mind: The Theory of Multiple Intelligence*, 3
George, Jean Craighead, list of author's books, 92
Gibbons, Gail, list of author's titles, 110
global knowledge, 6, 8–9
Goleman, D., *Emotional Intelligence*, 3
Gregoric, L., *Inside Styles: Beyond the Basics*, 3
group processing, 119–20
grouping chart, 66
grouping structures overview, 23–30
grouping without tracking. *See* tracking, grouping without
Grover, Max, *Accidental Zucchini, The: An Unexpected Alphabet*, 76–77
Grover, Max, *Circles and Squares Everywhere!*, 89
Guthrie, J., and A. Wigfield, *Reading Engagement: Motivating Readers Through Integrated Instruction*, 9

Hanly, Sheila, *Big Book of Animals, The*, 100–104, 109
Hest, Amy, *When Jessie Came Across the Sea*, 50
Hoban, Tana, *Is It Red? Is It Yellow? Is It Blue?*, 89
Horenstein, Henry, *A Is for . . .? A Photographer's Alphabet of Animals*, 88
Howe, James, *Return to Howliday Inn*, 92
humorous stories, books containing, 91
Hurwitz, Johanna, *Hot and Cold Summer, The*, 91

immigration, texts on, 49–50
independent learning/organization, list of resources, 131
independent work structures, gradually introducing, 120
individualized instruction, 24, 123
inquiry approaches, list of resources, 132
intensive intervention, reducing the need for, 123
intervention plan, sample response to, 124
Isadora, Rachel, *ABC Pop!*, 76–77
issues, in differentiating instruction
  helping others to understand, 126–27
  knowing if done effectively, 123–25
  putting together the four models, 121–23
  small groups vs. rest of students, 112–16

students working in small groups on their own, 116–20
students working independently on their own, 120–21

Jenkins, Martin, *Ape*, 109
Jensen, E., *Introduction to Brain-Compatible Learning*, 1
jigsawing
  general teaching suggestions, 53–56
  intermediate grade lesson, illustration of, 63–67
  lesson plan form, 137
  overview, 26
  primary lesson, illustration of, 57–62
  scenario and explanation, 51–53

key elements. *See* elements, key
Kirk, David, *Miss Spider's ABC*, 88
knowledge, local, global, and affective, 6–14
Kolb, D., *Experiential Learning: Experience as the Source of Learning and Development*, 3
Kucer, S., *Dimensions of Literacy: A Conceptual Base for Teaching Reading and Writing in School Settings*, 3

learning centers, list of resources, 132
learning styles, differentiation, 3
lesson plans
  connected literature circles, 76–77, 83–84
  focused readers' workshop, 101–102, 105–106
  form, 135
  grouping without tracking, 38–39, 44–45
  jigsawing, 58–59, 64–65
Lester, Alison, *Alice and Aldo*, 76–77
Levy, Elizabeth, *My Life as a Fifth Grade Comedian*, 91
literature circles, connected. *See* connected literature circles
literature response journal, T-chart for, 85
local knowledge, 6–8
Luenn, Nancy, *Celebration of Light*, 57–62

MacDonald, Suse, *Sea Shapes*, 90
MacLachlan, Sarah, *Sarah Plain and Tall*, 81–87
Manes, Stephen, *Be a Perfect Person in Just Three Days!*, 91
Markle, Sandra, *Growing Up Wild . . .* titles, 110
Markle, Sandra, *Snakes Biggest! Littlest!*, 111
Martin, Bill Jr., *Brown Bear, Brown Bear, What Do You See?*, 89
Martin, James, *Frogs*, 110

McArthur, Nancy, *Plant That Ate Dirty Socks, The*, 91

McCarthy, B., *Teaching Around the 4MAT Cycle: Designing Instruction for Diverse Learners with Diverse Learning Styles*, 3

McKeown, R., and J. Gentilucci, "Think-Aloud Strategy: Metacognitive Development and Monitoring Comprehension in the Middle School Second-Language Classroom," *Journal of Adolescent and Adult Literacy*, 17

McMillan, Bruce, *Wild Flamingos*, 111

Merriam, Eve, *Hole Story, The*, 89

Micklethwait, Lucy, *I Spy Colors in Art*, 89

mixed achievement, 28–29

models chart, grouping, 26

models, workshop. *See* workshop models

monitoring interaction patterns, 118–19

Morrison, Gordon, *Bald Eagle*, 109

mystery, books about, 92

Naidoo, Beverly, *Journey to Jo'burg*, 90

National Association of State Directors of Special Education (NASDE), 14

Neitzel, Shirley, *Bag I'm Taking to Grandma's, The*, 48

Opitz, M., and M. Ford, *Books and Beyond: New Ways to Reach Readers*, 9, 13, 24, 27–28, 112

options, in differential instruction, 114–16, 124

Paratore, Jean, *Classroom Contexts for Literacy Training: Flexible Grouping*, 32

Parsons, Alexandra, *Amazing Spiders*, 109

partners instruction, 24

Patent, Dorothy Hinshaw, *Slinky Scaly Slithery Snakes*, 111

Paulsen, Gary, *Hatchet*, 92

Pearson, Deborah, *Alphabeep: A Zipping, Zooming ABC*, 88

pioneer life, books about, 81–87

planning for different group sizes chart, 24

Pressley, M., *Reading Instruction That Works: The Case for Balanced Teaching*, 8, 27

Pringle, Laurence, *Crows! Strange and Wonderful*, 110

professional resources, list of, 129–33

questions, about these. *See* issues, in differentiating instruction

random assignments, for working in groups, 117

Rash, Andy, *Agent A to Agent Z*, 88

reader affect profiles, 12, 26

reader differentiation during reading instruction, 4

reader strategy profile charts, 10–11

readers differ and teachers matter, understanding how

differentiated instruction, what it is, 1–4

our beliefs about, 4–22

readers' workshop model, focused, 26, 96

reading and responding

connected literature circles, 73–74, 77, 79–80, 84, 86

directions for continued, 42

explanation of, 25

grouping without tracking, 35–36, 38–39, 41–42, 45, 47

jigsawing, 56, 58, 60–61, 63–66

questions to consider, 125

reminders, 29

workshop, focused readers', 99, 101–103, 105–108

reading performance patterns chart, 7

Reed, B., and J. Railsbeck, *Strategies and Resources of Mainstream Teachers of English Language Learners*, 17

Reilly Giff, Patricia, *Laura Ingalls Wilder*, 91

Reilly Giff, Patricia, list of author's books, 49–50

Reilly Giff, Patricia, *Nory Ryan's Song*, 33, 43–48, 113

reminders

for three-part lesson plan chart, 29

for working in groups, 117

responding. *See* reading and responding

Response to Intervention (RTI), 2, 14–16, 123, 124

Reutzel, D. R., and R. Cooter, 95

Roop, Connie, and Peter Roop, *Tales of Famous Americans*, 68

Rotner, Shelley, *Action Alphabet*, 88

Rounds, Glen, *Beaver*, 109

Rowland, Della, *Whales and Dolphins*, 63–67

Ruckman, Ivy, *Night of the Twisters*, 90

Ryder, Joanne, *Jaguar in the Rainforest*, 110

Rylant, Cynthia, *When I Was Young in the Mountain*, 84

Sabuda, Robert, *ABC Disney: An Alphabet Pop-Up*, 76–78

Sachar, Louis, *Dogs Don't Tell Jokes*, 91

Sandler, Martin, *Island of Hope: The Journey to America and the Ellis Island Experience*, 50

Schwartz, P., and P. Kluth, *You're Welcome: Differentiating Instruction in the Inclusive Classroom*, 1–2

semantic features grid, 62

Serfozo, Mary, *Who Said Red?*, 89
shapes, books about, 89–90
Silver, H., R. Strong, and M. Perini, *So Each May Learn: Integrating Learning Styles and Multiple Intelligences*, 3
similar achievement, 28–29
Simon, Charnan, *Jane Addams: Social Worker*, 91
Simon, Seymour, *Animals Nobody Loves*, 68
Simon, Seymour, *Crocodiles and Alligators*, 110
Simon, Seymour, *Penguins*, 110
Slate, Alfred, *Finding Buck Henry*, 92
small-group instruction, 24, 122–23
Snyder, Zilpha Keatley, *Gypsy Game, The*, 92
Sobel, June, *B Is for Bulldozer: A Construction ABC*, 88
sociocultural context chart, 5
special learners, list of resources for teaching, 133
Sternberg, R., *Successful Intelligence: How Practical and Creative Intelligence Determine Success in Life*, 3
Stine, Megan, *Story of Laura Ingalls Wilder, Pioneer Girl, The*, 81–87
Stolz, Mary, *Bully of Barkham Street, The*, 91
survival, books about, 92

Taylor, B., P. D. Pearson, K. Clark, and S. Walpole, "Effective School and Accomplished Teachers: Lesson About Primary Grade Reading Instruction in Low-Income Schools," *Elementary School Journal*, 21
teachers matter and readers differ, understanding how. *See* readers differ and teachers matter, understanding how
text differentiation during reading instruction, 4–5
text response, group chart across, 87
thinking styles, differentiation, 3
THNK (Things I Now Know), 67
Thompson, Lauren, *Apple Pie That Papa Baked, The*, 48
Tildes, Phyllis Limbacher, *Animals Black and White*, 109
Tomlinson, C., *Differentiated Classroom, The: Responding to the Needs of All Learners*, 1–2
tracking, grouping without
    general teaching suggestions, 34–36
    intermediate grade lesson, illustration of, 43–48

lesson plan form, 136
overview, 26
primary lesson, illustration of, 36–43
scenario and explanation, 31–33

Valencia, S., and M. Buly, "Behind Test Scores: What Struggling Readers *Really* Need," *Reading Teacher, The*, 9
Van Draanen, Wendelin, *Sammy Keyes and the Skeleton Man*, 92

Wagner, Jane, *J. T.*, 91
Wallace, Karen, *Gentle Giant Octopus*, 110
Walpole, S., and M. McKenna, *Differentiated Reading Instructions: Strategies for the Primary Grades*, 1
Wegman, William, *William Wegman ABC*, 89
westward expansion, books about, 81–87
Wharton-McDonald, R., M. Pressley, and J. M. Hampston, "Literacy Instruction in Nine First-Grade Classrooms: Teacher Characteristics and Student Achievement," *Elementary School Journal, The*, 21
Whelan, Gloria, *Wanigan, The: A Life on the River*, 81–87
whole-group instruction, 24, 121–22
Williams, Laura, *ABC Kids*, 88
Winebrenner, S., *Teaching Gifted Kids in the Regular Classroom: Strategies and Techniques Every Teacher Can Use to Meet the Academic Needs of the Gifted and Talented*, 115
WINK (What I Need to Know), 67
women, famous, books about, 90–91
Wood, Audrey, *Deep Blue Sea, The: A Book of Colors*, 89
workshop, focused readers'
    general teaching suggestions, 98–100
    intermediate grade lesson, illustration of, 104–109
    lesson plan form, 139
    overview, 26
    primary lesson, illustration of, 100–104
    scenario and explanation, 93–97
workshop models
    connected literature circles, 72
    focused readers', 96
    grouping without tracking, 33
    jigsawing, 54
Wormeli, R., *Differentiation: From Planning to Practice Grades 6–12*, 4